THE CREATIVE
Fish & Seafood
COOKBOOK

COURAGE
BOOKS
AN IMPRINT OF RUNNING PRESS
PHILADELPHIA • LONDON

Watercolor illustrations by Sally Damant
Designed by Stonecastle Graphics
Edited by Jillian Stewart

4526
© 1997 CLB International
All rights reserved under the Pan-American and International Copyright
Conventions. This edition first published in the United States in 1997 by
Courage Books

Printed in Singapore

9 8 7 6 5 4 3 2 1
Digit on the right indicates the number of this printing
Library of Congress Cataloging-in-Publication Number 96-71948
ISBN 0-7624-0099-4

This book was produced by CLB International, Godalming, Surrey, U.K.

Published by Courage Books, an imprint of
Running Press Book Publishers
125 South Twenty-second Street
Philadelphia, Pennsylvania 19103-4399

Contents

Introduction

America has long been blessed with an abundant supply of fish and seafood. The plentiful waters of the Atlantic, for instance, once provided not only a seemingly endless supply of salmon for the early settlers, but the clams and oysters that were such an important part of the Native Americans' diet. Today, although stocks have been depleted by over-fishing and pollution, we still have some of the best fishing grounds, with New England in particular renowned the world over for its fine seafood.

The current emphasis on light and nutritious meals has raised the appeal of fish and seafood. Obviously they have always been popular in areas where they are readily available, but they are now becoming a regular part of people's diet all over the country. Dietary advice to cut down on our fat intake has also been an important factor in encouraging people to turn to fish, in particular, as an alternative to red meat. Fish is an excellent source of protein and is considerably less fatty than most meats. Lean fish – cod, sole, and sea bass, for instance – contain practically no fat, while oily fish, such as mackerel, trout, and sardines, although a little more fatty, actually contain the type of fatty acids doctors believe may help prevent heart disease. Fish is also a good source of vitamins; oily fish, for instance, is particularly high in vitamins A and D, thiamin, and riboflavin.

Today, the majority of stores have a wider variety of fish than ever before and although this is long overdue, it can be rather daunting making a choice from such a wide variety. Perhaps the simplest way to approach this is to look at which category the fish fall into, as this gives a good hint as to how it should be treated.

All fish are either lean or oily. Lean fish have a distinctive white flesh and a mild flavor that is best treated very simply or complemented by a subtle sauce. Oily fish, in contrast, usually has a gray or red tinge and a much richer flavor that combines well with a robust accompaniment. Shellfish seems to have finally left behind its reputation for being difficult to cook and this too is now much more widely available in all its different guises.

The one crucial factor that should always be considered when preparing a dish of fish or shellfish is freshness. To obtain maximum results you need the freshest produce available: if the fish or shellfish are past their best then the end result will be disappointing. If you are lucky enough to live close to the ocean then finding a good supplier is relatively easy. If, however, you live far from such places, finding a consistently good supply can be difficult. Obviously getting fresh produce into the stores is a problem, although improved transportation and refrigeration have helped this immensely, but so too is fish that sits around in the supermarket waiting to be sold. A supplier with a fast turnover is therefore essential.

When choosing fresh fish look for signs that it really is fresh – moist flesh, bright eyes, red gills, and bright scales are all prerequisites, as is a lack of any unpleasant odor. Shellfish deteriorates even more rapidly than fish and checking for freshness is not quite as easy because the flesh is contained in the shell. However,

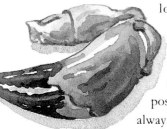

odor is a good giveaway as fresh shellfish should have no odor whatsoever. In addition, check that the shell looks fresh and moist; once it is past its best it will start to look dry and rather dull. Having bought your fresh produce from the supermarket, it still needs to be treated with care to retain its freshness until it reaches the pan. If possible, fresh fish and shellfish should always be bought on the day it is to be eaten. If this is not possible, store the fish in the refrigerator in a lidded container and use as soon as possible. Shellfish should be kept loosely wrapped in the refrigerator and used within a day.

If fresh fish and seafood are unavailable or are below par, then frozen produce is a good alternative. Fish and shellfish are, in theory, frozen as soon as they are caught to preserve their freshness, but obviously it more difficult to judge the freshness of a frozen product. Frozen fish are also usually cleaned before being frozen, an advantage for those who are reluctant to do this themselves.

Fish and seafood are quite rightly beginning to regain a position of importance in the American diet and their versatility should ensure that, unlike some trends that have come and gone, fish and seafood become a regular feature of our weekly menus.

Appetizers

Given the wide variety of seafood available it is little wonder that some of the world's favorite appetizers feature this most delicious of ingredients. Such delights as Moules Marinière from France and our own Oysters Rockefeller are testimony to the fact that seafood has a special part to play in numerous cuisines. Obviously those countries which are land-locked tend to lack seafood recipes, but in their place we find recipes utilizing any freshwater fish that are available.

Despite the ever-increasing sales of fish and seafood, many people are still a little unsure of quite how to prepare it. Rather than reject it altogether, however, it would seem that many choose instead to play safe by preparing a seafood appetizer, rather than feature it as an entrée. This approach is useful for inexperienced cooks as it allows them to become confident in handling and preparing fish and seafood without the worry of it being the main feature of a meal. The sheer number of seafood recipes from around the world also gives the cook the opportunity to try a wide variety of recipes, from traditional favorites such as Crab Meat Mousse to exciting dishes from the East such as Strawberry Shrimp or Fish Tempura, or contemporary recipes such as Shrimp and Avocado Cocktail or Anchovy Pâté with Crudité which appeal to our love of fresh light foods.

In addition to the diversity possible with seafood, it has the added advantage of being quick and easy to prepare. By its very nature seafood is best when lightly cooked: overcooking is the worst thing anyone can do to a seafood dish. It can, of course, take time to prepare an elaborate pâté, for instance, but it is the preparation that takes time and not the cooking so such dishes can often be prepared a little while before they are to be cooked, setting the cook free to get on with other courses. The results that can be achieved with a seafood appetizer often far outweigh the effort required on the part of the cook. Familiar though we are becoming with seafood, a good seafood appetizer still impresses.

Depending upon where you live, fish and seafood can be very expensive and featuring it in the smaller quantities required for an appetizer is the ideal way of getting round this. In addition, you can often buy trimmings which are especially good for making mousses and pâté – salmon trimmings are particularly good for this, given the expense of buying a whole fish. If you are looking for good value for money, look out for fresh fish in season; although some frozen fish and seafood can seem cheaper it will not compare with the quality of really fresh fish.

Serving a seafood appetizer is an excellent way of making your guests feel special and in this chapter you will find something for every occasion, whether you are having an elaborate dinner party or a family meal. With dishes as diverse as Garlic Fried Scallops, Mussels à la Genovese, and Crab Meat Mousse you will find being creative with fish and seafood is surprisingly simple.

Smoked Salmon Mousse

This light and attractive appetizer is perfect for dinner parties.

SERVES 4

¼ pound smoked salmon

2½ cups mayonnaise

1 Tbsp powdered gelatin

Lemon juice

¼ cup heavy cream

1 Tbsp all-purpose flour

1 Tbsp butter

¾ cup milk

1 egg white

1 small cucumber

1 jar red caviar

1 bunch watercress

1 small head iceberg lettuce

Salt and pepper

Lightly oil custard cups or small individual molds. Mix the lemon juice with enough water to make 3 tablespoons, and dissolve gelatin in the liquid. Warm the gelatin through gently to melt. Prepare sauce by melting butter and, when foaming, adding flour. Stir together well and blend in the milk gradually. Put back on the heat, stir continuously, and bring to a boil to thicken. Allow to cool slightly.

Chop the smoked salmon roughly and put into a food processor bowl with half the mayonnaise. Add seasonings and prepared sauce. Process until smooth and, with machine still running, pour in the melted gelatin. Pour in cream and process briefly. Set mixture over ice or in a cool place until thickening.

When thickened, whisk egg white until stiff but not dry, and fold into salmon mousse mixture. Put mixture into individual molds and chill until firm.

Meanwhile, prepare green mayonnaise. Pick over the watercress leaves, wash them well, remove thick stalks and the root ends. Chop the leaves roughly and put into food processor bowl. Add remaining prepared mayonnaise, seasoning, and lemon juice to taste, and process until well blended and a good green color. Spread mayonnaise onto individual serving plates. When mousse is chilled and set, turn out on top of green mayonnaise. Garnish the plate with shredded lettuce and decorate the top of each mousse with a thin slice of cucumber and a little red caviar.

Time: Preparation takes 20 minutes and cooking takes 5 minutes.

Anchovy Pâté with — Crudités —

Crudités are always a popular appetizer and make perfect finger food for parties.

SERVES 4

8 oz canned anchovies
¼ cup olive oil
3 oz package cream cheese
½ cup pitted black olives
2 Tbsps capers
1 Tbsp Dijon mustard
1 tsp ground pepper

Put all the ingredients into the bowl of a blender or food processor and run the machine until well mixed. The mixture may have to be worked in 2 batches. Serve with French bread or toast, and raw vegetables of all kinds – tomatoes, mushrooms, celery, radishes, green beans, cauliflower, carrots, cucumber, bell peppers, green onions, or quarters of hard-cooked eggs.
Time: Preparation takes 15 minutes.
Variation: Try making this dish with other canned oily fish such as sardines.

Crab Molds

Crab meat is spiced up with cayenne and mustard in this quickly prepared recipe.

SERVES 4

¾ cup cheddar cheese
¾ cup Parmesan cheese
1½ cups fresh white bread crumbs
1¼ cups cream
1 cup crab meat
3 eggs
1 tsp Worcestershire sauce
Cayenne pepper
Ground mace
Dry mustard
Salt and pepper

Separate the eggs and grate the cheese. Mix the bread crumbs with the cream and grated cheese. Add the Worcestershire sauce, a pinch of mace, Cayenne, dry mustard, and seasoning. Beat in the egg yolks. Whip the whites until stiff but not dry and fold into the cheese mixture along with the crab meat. Pour into a large, buttered, ovenproof pan or smaller custard cups. Bake in a preheated 425°F oven for about 15 minutes or until risen.
Time: Preparation takes 10 minutes and cooking takes 15 minutes.
Serving Idea: If using custard cups, serve the crab molds accompanied with a small leaf salad and lightly toasted bread.

Broiled Oysters

This simple treatment accentuates the flavor of the oysters perfectly.

SERVES 4

24 oysters

2 Tbsps butter

1¼ cups heavy cream

1 small jar red caviar

Salt and pepper

Tabasco sauce

Garnish

Watercress

Open the oysters using an oyster knife and leave them in their half-shells. Put a drop of Tabasco sauce on each oyster, season, then spoon over 2 teaspoons of heavy cream. Melt the butter and sprinkle it over the oysters. Put the oysters under a hot broiler for 2-3 minutes until lightly browned. When cooked, top each one with 1 teaspoon of red caviar, and serve with bouquets of watercress as a garnish.

Time: Preparation takes 10 minutes and cooking takes 2-3 minutes.

Cook's Tip: To open oysters, use a special oyster knife with a short, strong blade. Insert the knife at the hinge and twist until the shells separate.

Strawberry Shrimp

This dish will be enjoyed by both adults and children.

SERVES 4

¾ pound shrimp, shelled and minced

1 small can water chestnuts, peeled and minced

½ cup ham, ground

1 tsp white wine

¼ tsp finely chopped green onion

¼ tsp grated fresh ginger root

1½ Tbsps cornstarch

1 egg white

Sesame seeds

Pinch of salt

Oil for deep frying

4 Tbsps hoisin sauce

1 tsp white or rice wine vinegar

1 tsp honey

2 Tbsps water

1 tsp sesame oil

Mix the shrimp and water chestnuts with the wine, green onion, ginger, egg white, and a pinch of salt. Chill the mixture for 30 minutes before using. Form the mixture into strawberry-sized balls and cover each ball with the finely ground ham. Heat the oil to 375°F and deep-fry the balls for 3 minutes, or until crisp. Drain, roll in sesame seeds to coat, and place on a plate. Mix the hoisin sauce, honey, vinegar, water, and sesame oil together, and serve with the shrimp balls.

Time: Preparation takes 10 minutes and cooking takes 3 minutes.

Goujons

Always a great favorite goujons, served with a variety of sauces, are suitable for a host of different occasions.

SERVES 4

2 sole
Seasoned all-purpose flour
1 egg
2 tsps olive oil
Dry bread crumbs
Oil for deep frying
Pinch of salt

Tartare sauce
2 Tbsps mayonnaise
1 Tbsp heavy cream
2 tsps chopped fresh parsley
2 tsps chopped dill pickles
2 tsps chopped capers
1 tsp chopped onion

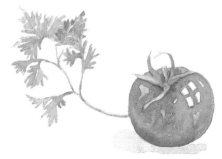

Curry sauce
2 Tbsps mayonnaise
1 Tbsp heavy cream
1 tsp curry powder
1½ tsps mango relish

Tomato herb sauce
2 Tbsps mayonnaise
1 Tbsp heavy cream
1 tsp chopped fresh parsley
1 tsp chopped fresh tarragon
1 tsp chopped chives
1 tsp tomato paste
Squeeze of lemon

Fillet the sole and skin the fillets. Rinse the fillets in cold water and pat dry. Cut each fillet on the diagonal into pieces about ½-inch thick and 2½-3-inches long. Coat thoroughly with seasoned flour, shaking off any excess. Beat the eggs lightly and mix in the olive oil. Dip fish pieces into the mixture and roll them in the bread crumbs. Put fish aside in a cool place: do not coat the fish too soon before cooking. Mix the ingredients for each sauce together and set aside. Heat the oil in a deep fryer to about 375°F. Put fish into the frying basket and lower into the hot oil. Fry for 2-3 minutes until crisp and golden brown. Fry in small batches. Drain fish on paper towels, sprinkle lightly with salt, and then pile the fish into a hot serving dish. Garnish with wedges of lemon and sprigs of parsley, if desired, and serve the sauces separately for dipping the fish.
Time: Preparation takes 20-30 minutes and cooking takes 2-3 minutes.

Moules Marinière

Brittany and Normandy are famous for mussels and for cream and so cooks combined the two in one perfect seafood dish.

SERVES 4

3 pounds mussels
1½ cups dry cider or white wine
4 shallots, finely chopped
1 clove garlic, finely chopped
1 bouquet garni
½ cup heavy cream
3 Tbsps butter, cut into small pieces
2 Tbsps finely chopped fresh parsley

Scrub the mussels well and remove the beards and any barnacles from the shells. Discard any mussels that have cracked shells and do not open when lightly tapped. Put the mussels into a bowl and soak in cold water for at least 1 hour.

Meanwhile, chop the parsley very finely. Bring the cider or wine to a boil in a large pan and add the shallots, garlic, and bouquet garni. Add the mussels, cover the pan and cook for 5 minutes. Shake the pan or stir the mussels around frequently until the shells open. Lift out the mussels into a large soup tureen or individual serving bowls. Discard any mussels that have not opened. Boil the cooking liquid to reduce it by about half then strain into another saucepan. Add the cream and bring to a boil to thicken slightly. Beat in the butter, a few pieces at a time. Adjust the seasoning, add the parsley, and pour the sauce over the mussels to serve.

Time: Preparation takes about 30 minutes and cooking takes about 15 minutes.

Preparation: Soak mussels with a handful of flour or cornmeal in the water. They will then expel sand and take up the flour or cornmeal, which plumps them up.

Fried Squid

Squid was once caught off the New England coast and taken to Mediterranean countries where it is a great favorite. Nowadays it's a popular food here, too.

SERVES 4

1½ pounds squid, cleaned and cut into rings

½ cup all-purpose flour

Salt and pepper

Oil for deep frying

Lemon wedges and fresh parsley for garnishing

Mix the flour, salt, and pepper together on a sheet of wax paper or in a shallow dish. Toss the rings of squid in the flour mixture to coat. Heat the oil to 350°F and fry the squid, about 6 pieces at a time.

Remove them from the oil when brown and crisp and place on paper towels. Sprinkle lightly with salt and continue with the remaining squid. The pieces will take about 3 minutes to cook. Place on serving dishes and garnish each dish with a wedge of lemon and some parsley.

Time: Preparation takes 25 minutes and cooking takes 3 minutes per batch of 6.

Cook's Tip: Be careful not to overcook the squid as this will make it tough.

Crab Smithfield

Virginia's famous Smithfield ham makes a wonderful addition to fresh crab meat in this quickly-made first course.

SERVES 2-4

1 oz butter

5 oz crab meat

1 oz Smithfield ham, cut into julienne slices

Garnish

Parsley sprigs

Lemon wedges

Melt the butter in a sauté pan. Add the crab meat and sauté for 2 minutes. Arrange the julienned ham on top and brown under the broiler for 1 minute. Garnish with sprigs of parsley and a lemon wedge before serving.

Time: Preparation takes 5 minutes and cooking takes about 3 minutes.

Buying Guide: Fresh crab meat can usually be bought from the fish market. Use it on the day of purchase.

Oysters Rockefeller

The sauce in this recipe was said to be as rich as Rockefeller, hence the name.

24 oysters, on the half shell

Rock salt

6 strips bacon, finely chopped

1¼ pounds fresh spinach, washed and leaves finely chopped

1 small bunch green onions, finely chopped

2 cloves garlic, finely chopped

4-5 Tbsps fine fresh bread crumbs

Dash of Tabasco sauce

2 Tbsps aniseed liqueur

Pinch of salt

Parmesan cheese

Loosen the oysters from their shells using a knife, strain and reserve their liquid. Rinse the shells well and return an oyster to each one. Pour about 1 inch of rock salt into a baking pan and place in the oysters in their shells, pressing each shell gently into the salt. Place the bacon in a large skillet and cook slowly to render it. Turn up the heat and brown the bacon evenly. Add the spinach, green onions, and garlic, and cook slowly until softened. Add the bread crumbs, Tabasco sauce, oyster liquid, liqueur, and a pinch of salt. Spoon some of the mixture onto each oyster and sprinkle with Parmesan cheese. Cook in a preheated 350°F oven for 10 minutes, or until golden, and then place under a preheated broiler to lightly brown the cheese.

Time: Preparation takes 25 minutes and cooking takes about 25 minutes.

Shrimp Cocktail

If available, use jumbo shrimp for this tasty recipe.

SERVES 4

5-6 lettuce leaves

½ pound cooked, shelled shrimp

Chopped fresh parsley

4 lemon wedges

Cocktail sauce

4 heaped Tbsps mayonnaise

2 Tbsps tomato paste

1 tsp Worcestershire sauce

2 tsps lemon juice

4 tsps medium sherry

2 Tbsps whipping cream

To make the sauce, add the paste, Worcestershire sauce, lemon juice, and sherry to the mayonnaise and mix well. Fold in the whipped cream. Shred the lettuce finely and divide between four glass goblets. Reserve 4 shrimp, and divide the remaining shrimp between the 4 goblets. Just before serving, coat the shrimp with the cocktail sauce and sprinkle a pinch of the chopped parsley on top of each. Garnish with a jumbo shrimp and a lemon wedge on each glass.

Time: Preparation takes 15 minutes.

Cook's Tip: This is a great appetizer to serve at large dinner parties, as it can be prepared earlier in the day and simply constructed just before serving.

Pâté of Salmon & — Scallops —

This impressive appetizer will please the most discerning of guests.

SERVES 4

¾ pound salmon
1 pound haddock or other whitefish
5 scallops with roe attached
1¼ cups heavy cream
3 eggs
1 Tbsp chopped fresh parsley
1 Tbsp chopped fresh tarragon
1 Tbsp lemon juice
1 Tbsp dry white wine
½ cup unsalted butter
Salt and pepper
Pinch of cayenne pepper

Separate the eggs and set aside the yolks. Remove skin and bone from salmon and haddock. Put the salmon into a food processor bowl with half the egg whites and half the cream. Season and process until smooth. Put into a separate bowl, and repeat the process with the haddock. Lightly butter a 2 pound loaf pan. Put half of haddock mixture into the bottom of the pan and smooth out. Cover with half of the salmon mixture. Clean the scallops and separate the roe from the white part. Cut white part in half through the middle. Chop the roe coarsely and put it down the center of the salmon mixture. Place the rounds of white scallops on either side of the roe. Put another layer of salmon mixture over, and then the remaining haddock mixture on top and smooth out. Cover well with double thickness of buttered foil. Put into a roasting pan and fill it halfway up with hand-hot water. Bake the pâté in a preheated 350°F oven for about 1 hour, or until firm.

Meanwhile, prepare a quick Bernaise sauce. Put the reserved egg yolks into a food processor bowl or blender. Chop the herbs coarsely and add to the egg yolks along with cayenne pepper, pinch of salt, lemon juice, and white wine. Process until mixed thoroughly and the herbs are chopped. Melt the butter and, when foaming, turn on machine and pour the melted butter through the feed tube very gradually. This will cook the egg yolks and the sauce will thicken. Keep warm in a double boiler. When pâté has finished cooking, allow to cool slightly in the pan. Gently turn the fish pâté out and cut into 1-inch thick slices. Arrange on serving plates and pour over some of the Bernaise sauce. Serve the rest of the sauce separately.

Time: Preparation takes 30 minutes and cooking takes 1 hour.

Fish Tempura

This is a traditional Japanese dish, which can be served as an unusual appetizer.

SERVES 4

12 uncooked large shrimp
2 whitefish fillets, skinned and cut into 2 x ¾-inch strips
Small whole fish, e.g. whitebait
2 squid, cleaned and cut into strips 1x3 inches long
2 Tbsps all-purpose flour, for dusting
1 egg yolk
Scant ½ cup iced water
1 cup all-purpose flour
Oil for frying
6 Tbsps soy sauce
Juice and finely grated rind of 2 limes
4 Tbsps dry sherry

Shell the shrimp, leaving the tails intact. Wash the fish and the squid and pat dry. Dust them all with the 2 tablespoons flour. Make a batter by beating together the egg yolk and water. Sieve in the 1 cup of all-purpose flour and mix in well with a knife. Dip each piece of fish into the batter, shaking off any excess.

In a wok or deep-fat fryer, heat the oil to 350°F. Lower in the fish pieces a few at a time and cook for 2-3 minutes, or until crisp. Lift them out carefully and drain on paper towels, keeping warm until required. Mix together the soy sauce, lime juice, rind, and sherry and serve as a dip with the cooked fish.

Time: Preparation takes about 30 minutes and cooking takes 2-3 minutes.

Garlic Fried Scallops

Scallops are regarded by many chefs as the best shellfish available for their lovely flavor. This recipe lets all the flavor shine through.

SERVES 4

16 scallops
1 large clove garlic, finely chopped
4 Tbsps butter
3 Tbsps chopped fresh parsley
2 lemons
Seasoned all-purpose flour

Rinse scallops and remove black veins. If scallops are large, cut in half horizontally. Squeeze the juice from 1 lemon. Sprinkle the scallops lightly with seasoned flour. Heat butter in a skillet and add chopped garlic and scallops. Fry until pale golden brown. Pour over the lemon juice, and cook to reduce the amount of liquid. Toss in the chopped parsley. Pile the scallops into individual scallop shells or porcelain baking dishes. Keep warm, and garnish with lemon wedges before serving.

Time: Preparation takes 10 minutes and cooking takes 6-8 minutes.

Devilled Stuffed Crab

Use fresh crab meat for this recipe, if possible, as its flavor is superior to the canned variety.

SERVES 4

2 cooked crabs or 2 cups crab meat
¼ cup shelled pistachio nuts
2 hard-cooked eggs
1 Tbsp all-purpose flour
1 Tbsp butter
1¼ cups milk
1 green bell pepper
1 medium onion
2 Tbsps chili sauce or hamburger relish
2 tsps white wine vinegar
2 tsps chopped dill pickles
1 tsp Dijon mustard
½ tsp Worcestershire sauce
Tabasco sauce
3 Tbsps butter or margarine
4 Tbsps dry bread crumbs
Chopped fresh parsley
Salt and pepper
Garnish
Lemon wedges
Watercress

Buy the crabs already cleaned. If you wish to do it yourself, twist off all the legs, separate body from shell, and remove lungs and stomach. Cut body into 3 or 4 pieces with a sharp knife and pick out all the meat. Scrape brown meat from inside shell and crack large claws and remove meat. Add all this meat to the body meat. Crab shells may be washed and used to bake in.

Melt 1 tablespoon butter in a small saucepan. When foaming, take it off the heat and stir in flour, then the milk, gradually. Stir continuously, return to the heat and bring to a boil, allowing it to thicken. Set aside to cool slightly. Chop the egg roughly, and dice the green bell pepper and onion. Break up crab meat. Chop pistachio nuts, and add all other ingredients to the white sauce. Lightly butter the clean shell or individual baking dishes. Fill with crab meat mixture and top with dry crumbs. Melt 3 tablespoons butter and sprinkle over top of crumbs. Bake in a preheated 375°F oven for 15 minutes, and brown under broiler if necessary. Sprinkle with chopped parsley and garnish with lemon wedges and watercress.

Time: Preparation takes 10-15 minutes and cooking takes 20 minutes.

Mussels à la Genovese

There is a distinct hint of classic Italian flavors in this unusual recipe.

SERVES 4

1 quart mussels
Lemon juice
1 shallot, finely chopped
1 handful fresh basil leaves
1 small bunch fresh parsley
4-5 walnut halves
1 clove garlic
2 Tbsps fresh grated Parmesan cheese
3-6 Tbsps olive oil
2 Tbsps olive oil
2 Tbsps butter
Salt and pepper
Flour or oatmeal

Garnish
Fresh bay leaves or basil leaves

Scrub the mussels well and discard any with broken shells. Put mussels into a bowl of clean water with a handful of flour. Leave for 30 minutes, then rinse under clear water. Chop the shallot finely and place in a large saucepan with the lemon juice. Cook until the shallot softens. Add mussels and a pinch of salt and pepper, cover the pan and cook the mussels quickly, shaking the pan. When mussel shells have opened, take them out of the pan, set aside, and keep warm. Strain the cooking liquid for possible use later.

To prepare Genovese sauce, wash the basil leaves and parsley, peel the garlic clove and chop coarsely, and chop the walnuts coarsely. Put the herbs, garlic, nuts, 1 tablespoon grated cheese, and salt and pepper into a food processor and work to a coarse mixture. Add the butter and work again. Turn machine on and add oil gradually through the feed tube. If the sauce is still too thick, add the reserved liquid from cooking the mussels. Remove top shells from mussels and discard. Arrange mussels evenly in 4 shallow dishes, spoon some of the sauce into each, and sprinkle the top lightly with remaining Parmesan cheese. Garnish with bay or basil leaves and serve.

Time: Preparation takes 15 minutes and cooking takes about 6 minutes.

Fried Fish with Garlic Sauce

Tiny whole fish make an excellent first course.

SERVES 4

2 pounds fresh anchovies or whitebait
1 cup all-purpose flour
4-6 Tbsps cold water
Pinch of salt
Oil for frying

Garlic sauce
4 slices bread, crusts trimmed, soaked in water for 10 minutes
4 cloves garlic, peeled and coarsely chopped
2 Tbsps lemon juice
4-5 Tbsps olive oil
1-2 Tbsps water (optional)
Salt and pepper
2 tsps chopped fresh parsley
Lemon wedges for garnishing (optional)

Sift the flour into a deep bowl with a pinch of salt. Gradually stir in the water in the amount needed to make a very thick batter. Heat enough oil for frying in a large, deep skillet. Take 3 fish at a time and dip them into the batter together. Press their tails together firmly to make a fan shape. Lower them carefully into the oil. Fry in several batches until crisp and golden. Continue in the same way with all the remaining fish.

Meanwhile, squeeze out the bread and place in a food processor with the garlic and lemon juice. With the processor running, add the oil in a thin, steady stream. Add water if the mixture is too thick and dry. Add salt and pepper and stir in the parsley by hand. When all the fish are cooked, sprinkle lightly with salt and arrange on serving plates with some of the garlic sauce and lemon wedges, if desired.

Time: Preparation takes about 30 minutes and cooking takes about 3 minutes per batch for the fish.

Preparation: Coat the fish in the batter just before ready for frying.

Cook's Tip: The fish should be eaten immediately after frying. If it is necessary to keep the fish warm, place them on a wire cooling rack covered with paper towels in a slow oven with the door open.

Smoked Trout Pâté

Smoked fish is particularly well suited for making pâté.

SERVES 4

4 lemons
2 fillets or 1 whole smoked trout
6 Tbsps butter
8 oz package cream cheese
Lemon juice
Tabasco sauce
Ground nutmeg
Salt and pepper

Garnish

Fresh bay leaves

Cut the lemons in half and trim the ends so the shells sit upright. Scoop out the lemon flesh completely. Remove the skin and bones from the trout. Put fish into a food processor with the butter, cream cheese, seasoning, lemon juice, nutmeg, and Tabasco sauce and work until smooth. Put the pâté into a pastry bag fitted with a rose tube and pipe into the lemon shells. Garnish each with a bay leaf.

Time: Preparation takes 20 minutes.

Serving Idea: Serve with hot buttered toast and a mixture of peppery salad leaves.

Catfish Hors D'oeuvre

Catfish is a Southern speciality and many restaurants in the region feature it on their menus.

SERVES 18

1 cup yellow cornmeal
½ tsp garlic salt
½ tsp cayenne
4 catfish fillets, diced
Oil for frying

Combine the cornmeal, garlic salt, and cayenne pepper. Roll the diced catfish in this mixture to coat. Fry in oil which has been heated to 375°F, or until a 1-inch cube of bread browns in 1 minute. The fish pieces will sink to the bottom of the pan. When they rise to the surface they are done. The pieces should be golden brown. Drain on paper towels and serve hot.

Time: Preparation takes 20 minutes and cooking takes 15-20 minutes.

Variation: If catfish are not available substitute bullhead.

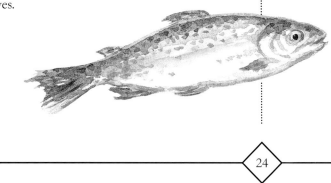

Shrimp & Avocado Cocktail

This colorful appetizer is perfect for a summer meal.

SERVES 4

8 oz cooked jumbo shrimp
2 oranges
2 large, ripe avocados
1 small Spanish onion or 2 green onions
¼ cup whipping cream
2 Tbsps ketchup
2 Tbsps mayonnaise
2 tsps lemon juice
12 black olives, pitted and sliced
2 tsps brandy
Pinch of cayenne pepper
Pinch of sugar
Salt and pepper
Lettuce

Peel the oranges over a bowl to reserve juice. Peel the cooked shrimp and set aside. To prepare the dressing, beat cream until thick, and mix with ketchup, mayonnaise, lemon juice, Cayenne, sugar, salt and pepper, brandy, and some of the reserved orange juice. The dressing should be slightly thick. Chop the onion finely. Cut avocados in half lengthwise and remove the stones. Peel them carefully and cut each half into 4-6 long slices. Shred the lettuce, arrange on serving dishes and place the avocado slices in a fan shape on top of the lettuce. Brush each slice lightly with orange juice to prevent it discoloring. Arrange an orange segment in between each slice. Pile the shrimp up at the top of the avocado fan and coat with some of the dressing. Garnish with olives and sprinkle over chopped onion.

Time: Preparation takes 20 minutes.

Crab Meat Mousse

Serve this delicious mousse with a small green side salad for a first course.

SERVES 4

1 pound crab meat, cooked and flaked

½ cup mayonnaise

⅔ cup whipping cream

2 Tbsps sherry

2 egg whites

2 tsps Dijon mustard

1 small bunch chives

1 Tbsp aspic powder

Juice of 1 lime or lemon

1 ripe avocado

1 Tbsp gelatin

Salt and pepper

Dissolve the gelatin in some of the lemon or lime juice. Warm gently to dissolve, and mix with mayonnaise, mustard, and salt and pepper to taste. Lightly whip the cream and fold into mayonnaise mixture along with crab meat. Put over ice or in a cool place until thickened, then whip the egg whites until stiff but not dry and fold into mixture. Quickly pour into a bowl or soufflé dish, smooth the top, and chill until set. Meanwhile, bring 1 cup water to a boil. Stir in sherry, add 1 tablespoon aspic powder and stir until dissolved. Allow to cool slightly. Chop the chives and add to aspic. When the mousse mixture is set, chill the aspic until it begins to thicken slightly. Pour about ¼-inch of the aspic over the top of the set mousse, and return to refrigerator to set the aspic. Cut avocado in half lengthwise and remove stone. Peel carefully and cut each half into thin slices. Brush with lemon juice and arrange slices on top of set aspic. Spoon over some of the aspic to set the avocado slices, and chill. When avocado is set, pour remaining aspic over to fill to the top of the dish, and chill until set.

Time: Preparation takes 30 minutes plus chilling time.

Oysters Casino

Oysters were once so plentiful that they played an important part in the staple diet of the poor.

SERVES 3-4

12 oysters

½ small green bell pepper, diced

½ small onion, diced

1 pinch seafood seasoning per oyster

2 drops lemon juice per oyster

½ cup Monterey Jack cheese, grated

3 strips bacon, cut into 1-inch pieces

To serve

Butter

Lemon wedges

Open the oysters using an oyster knife and loosen from the shells at the muscle. Place a small amount of finely diced bell pepper and onion on top of each and sprinkle with the seafood seasoning and lemon juice. Cover each oyster with grated Monterey Jack cheese and top with a piece of bacon. Bake at 350°F for 6-8 minutes, or until lightly browned. Serve with butter and lemon wedges.

Time: Preparation takes 15 minutes and cooking takes 6-8 minutes.

Stuffed Quahogs

Quahogs are hard-shell clams that are used for chowder when large, and eaten on the half shell when smaller.

SERVES 4

3 Tbsps butter

1 onion, chopped

1 green and 1 red bell pepper, chopped

1 clove garlic, finely chopped

¼ tsp oregano

8 quahogs, shelled, poached for 3 minutes and chopped

Fresh bread crumbs

4 tsps grated Romano or Parmesan cheese

Lemon wedges and hot pepper sauce to serve

Heat the butter in a pan and sauté the onion and peppers until softened, add the garlic and oregano; cook for another 1-2 minutes over a low heat. Stir in the chopped clams with an equal amount of fresh bread crumbs, and the cheese. Moisten with additional melted butter and/or clam juice. Stuff into each clam shell half and bake in a preheated 375°F oven for about 10 minutes until hot and slightly browned. Serve with lemon wedges and hot pepper sauce.

Time: Preparation takes 20 minutes and cooking takes 15 minutes.

Cook's Tip: To facilitate opening, place well-scrubbed clams in a pan in a moderate oven and heat until they open. Use a strong knife to pry off the top shells.

Soups & Stews

Mention soups and stews and an image of pans boiling away for hours comes to mind. While such an image may be appropriate for meat stews, most of which feature tough meat that requires slow cooking, it is certainly not appropriate for seafood. Seafood needs delicate treatment to prevent its tender flesh becoming dry and tough, and although it means the cook has to keep a careful eye on the pan, it also means that a delicious soup or stew can be produced in almost no time at all.

Add to this the fact that soups and stews are easy to prepare and exceptionally versatile, and you have the perfect dish for cooks of all abilities. It is often easiest to start off with a very plain dish that is not too difficult before progressing to some of the more complex and expensive recipes. It is actually quite difficult to make a soup or stew that is inedible, but it does take a little practice to produce one that is absolutely first-class. The range of ingredients that can be incorporated in a soup or stew is immense and it is all too easy to be tempted to think that the more ingredients there are the better the dish will taste. With seafood soups and stews this is simply not true. Some of the most impressive dishes are the very simple ones which allow all the flavor of the seafood to shine through. It is important to remember, however, that to produce a really stunning simple dish, the fish or seafood needs to be as fresh as possible; if it is not the result will be a dish with the undisguised flavor of old fish.

Soups and stews are very much alike; the main difference is that stews tend to be heartier and have less liquid. The adaptability of seafood is particularly evident in the number of exciting soup recipes from around the world, all with quite distinct flavors. In this chapter everything from a very light Crab and Watercress Soup from China and a sweet and spicy Coconut Shrimp Soup from Thailand, to a traditional Smoked Salmon Bisque and She-crab Soup, is featured. As well as these warming soups, why not try Chilled Shrimp and Avocado Soup – it's perfect for a hot summer's day.

Seafood stews have always been a great favorite as they can be adapted to suit whatever ingredients the cook has available. In the South, for instance, okra is a useful addition as it has a thick gluey sap that helps to thicken the stew. (Seafood stews do not thicken in the same way as meat stews because seafood does not contain the same amount of gelatin as meat.) Italian seafood stew, in contrast, contains the wonderful sunny ingredients, such as garlic, tomatoes, and olives, so quintessentially Mediterranean.

Once you become quite adept at producing stews from recipes, you can try concocting your own recipe. The basic rule is to make sure each ingredient is cooked for the correct amount of time and that they are not all thrown in together so that the fish is overcooked while the potatoes are still raw. Preparing soups and and stews is a great introduction to cooking with seafood and is particularly appropriate for entertaining, as the recipes can easily be adjusted to serve a crowd.

Mussel Soup

Crusty white bread is the perfect accompaniment for this soup.

SERVES 4

2 quarts fresh mussels
¼ cup butter
2 onions, finely chopped
2 cloves garlic, finely chopped
1¼ cups dry white wine
1¼ cups water
2 Tbsps lemon juice
1 cup fresh bread crumbs
2 Tbsps chopped fresh parsley
Salt and pepper

Scrub the mussels with a stiff brush and remove any barnacle shells or pieces of seaweed that are attached to them. Tap each mussel sharply and discard any that do not close tightly. Melt the butter in a large saucepan and gently fry the onions and garlic until soft, but not browned. Add the mussels, wine, water, and lemon juice to the pan, and bring to a boil. Season with salt and pepper, then cover and cook for approximately 10 minutes or until all the mussel shells have completely opened.

Discard any mussels that have not opened fully. Strain the mussels through a colander and return the juices and broth to the saucepan. Put the mussels in a serving tureen and keep warm. Add the bread crumbs and the parsley to the mussel juices and bring to a boil. Adjust the seasoning, and serve over the mussels in the tureen. Serve immediately.

Time: Preparation takes 15 minutes and cooking takes 20 minutes.

Solianka

Many people prefer to buy a ready-prepared fish broth, but making your own as the basis for a fish stew gives a far more authentic result.

SERVES 4

2 pounds fish bones
5 cups water
1 onion, coarsely chopped
1 stalk celery, coarsely chopped
1 carrot, coarsely chopped
1 bay leaf
1¼ cups canned tomatoes
1 small bunch green onions, chopped
4 small dill pickles, chopped
1 Tbsp chopped black olives
2 Tbsps capers
1½ pounds salmon or salmon trout
Salt and pepper
Garnish
⅔ cup sour cream
1 small jar black caviar

Cook the fish bones in the water with the onion, celery, and carrot. Add the bay leaf, and simmer for about 1 hour. Drain off the broth and reserve. Add tomatoes to the broth. Add the green onions, pickles, olives, and capers. Cut the salmon into 1-inch cubes, add to the broth, season and cover. Simmer for 10-12 minutes or until salmon is cooked. Serve the soup in warm serving dishes topped with sour cream and black caviar.
Time: Preparation takes 10 minutes and cooking takes 70 minutes.

Shrimp, Avocado & Cucumber Soup

Chilled soups make the perfect summer luncheon dish.

SERVES 4

8 oz unpeeled shrimp
1¼ cups chicken broth
1 large ripe avocado
1 small cucumber
1 small bunch dill
Juice of half a lemon
2½ cups plain yogurt
Salt and pepper

Peel all the shrimp, reserving shells. Add shells to chicken broth, bring to a boil and simmer for about 15 minutes. Cool and strain. Peel the avocado and cut it into pieces. Cut 8 thin slices from the cucumber and peel the rest. Remove seeds and chop the cucumber coarsely. Put avocado and cucumber into a food processor or blender and process until smooth. Add a squeeze of lemon juice, and strain on the cold chicken broth. Reserve a sprig of dill for garnish, and add the rest to the mixture in the processor and blend again. Add about 2 cups of yogurt to the processor and blend until smooth. Add salt and pepper. Stir in the peeled shrimp by hand. Chill the soup well. Serve in individual bowls, garnished with a spoonful of yogurt, a spring of dill, and thinly sliced rounds of cucumber.

Time: Preparation takes 15 minutes and cooking takes 15 minutes.

Florida Seafood Stew

Florida is justifiably famous for its seafood and this stew makes excellent use of the wide variety of seafood available.

SERVES 8-10

Fish broth

1 quart cold water

2 pounds fish bones and fish heads

2 onions, coarsely chopped

2 sprigs parsley, chopped

3-4 celery tops, coarsely chopped

Juice of ½ lemon

Salt and pepper

Stew

⅓ cup olive oil

1 Tbsp butter

1 Tbsp garlic, finely chopped

4 Tbsps onion, chopped

1 Tbsp fresh parsley, chopped

2 tomatoes, peeled, seeded and chopped

1 Tbsp tomato paste

Pinch thyme, saffron, and oregano

Salt and pepper

2-3 pounds fresh fish, boned and cut into chunks

2-3 pounds shellfish, such as lobster, shrimp, crab, clams or scallops, cleaned, but left in their shells

⅓ cup cognac or brandy

1½ cups dry white wine

First prepare the fish broth by combining the fish bones and heads with the water in a large pan. Bring to a boil and add the remaining ingredients. Simmer for 1 hour, skimming as necessary. Strain and set aside. To prepare the stew, heat the olive oil and butter in a large skillet. Add the garlic, onions, parsley, tomatoes, tomato paste, and seasonings. Sauté for 3-4 minutes, then add the fish and shellfish. Stir and cook for another 1-2 minutes. Pour the cognac over the seafood. Ignite and allow to flame briefly. Transfer the stew to a stew pot, and add the white wine and the fish broth. Simmer for 10 minutes before serving. Discard any shellfish whose shells have not opened.

Time: Preparation takes 45 minutes and cooking takes 1 hour 15 minutes.

Shrimp Bisque

This classic Cajun recipe owes its origin to the French settlers.

SERVES 6

3 Tbsps butter or margarine
1 onion, finely chopped
1 red bell pepper, finely chopped
2 stalks celery, finely chopped
1 clove garlic, finely chopped
Pinch dry mustard and cayenne pepper
2 tsps paprika
3 Tbsps all-purpose flour
4 cups fish broth
1 sprig thyme and a bay leaf
8 oz raw, peeled shrimp
Salt and pepper
Snipped chives

Melt the butter or margarine in a saucepan. Add the onion, bell pepper, celery, and garlic. Cook gently to soften. Stir in the mustard, cayenne, paprika, and flour. Cook about 3 minutes over gentle heat, stirring occasionally. Pour on the broth gradually, stirring until well blended. Add the thyme and bay leaf and bring to a boil. Reduce the heat and simmer about 5 minutes or until thickened, stirring occasionally. Add the shrimp and cook gently until pink and curled – about 5 minutes. Season with salt and pepper to taste, remove the bay leaf and top with snipped chives before serving.

Time: Preparation takes 20 minutes and cooking takes 8-10 minutes.

Livernese Fish Soup

A very tasty, slightly spicy fish soup. Great for cold winter evenings.

SERVES 4

3½ pounds fish (small whole fish and a little shellfish), cleaned
1 onion, sliced
1 carrot, sliced
Small bunch fresh parsley, well rinsed and dried
1 small chili pepper, seeded and chopped
3 cloves garlic
½ cup white wine
4 tomatoes, quartered
1 stick French bread
3 Tbsps olive oil
½ cup finely grated Parmesan cheese
Salt and pepper

Heat the olive oil in a large pan and gently fry the carrots, onion, chili pepper, and parsley. Add the fish and shellfish and continue frying for 4 minutes. Deglaze the pan with the dry white wine and stir in the garlic and tomatoes. Stir well and continue cooking for a few minutes, then pour over plenty of water. Bring to a boil, reduce the heat and simmer for 1 hour. Adjust seasoning as necessary. Cut the French stick into slices and toast them. Strain the soup through a fine sieve. Serve the soup piping hot spooned over the toasted bread and sprinkled with the cheese.

Time: Preparation takes about 15 minutes and total cooking time is about 1 hour and 30 minutes.

Fish Soup with Surprise — Wontons —

Chinese ravioli stuffed with shrimp and cooked in a fish-flavored soup.

SERVES 4

3 cups fish broth

12 shrimp, peeled and heads removed, peelings and heads set aside

1 Tbsp oil

½ tsp chopped fresh parsley

Pinch of chopped garlic

Salt and pepper

12 wonton wrappers

1 egg, beaten

1 Tbsp soy sauce

Bring the fish broth to a boil together with the reserved heads and peelings from the shrimp. Boil gently for 15 minutes. Strain through a fine sieve, reserving only the broth. Heat the oil in a wok and stir-fry four of the shrimp, cut into small pieces, together with the parsley, garlic, and salt and pepper to taste. Allow to cool. Spread out the wonton wrappers and place a little of the above stuffing on each one. Brush the beaten egg all around the edges of the dough. Fold one side over onto the other, cut the ravioli into the desired shape and seal well by pinching the edges together firmly. Set the ravioli aside to rest for 10 minutes.

Bring the stock back to a boil, then add the remaining shrimp and the soy sauce. Pinch once more round the edges of the ravioli, then slip them into the broth. Season with salt and pepper and simmer briskly for 5 minutes. Serve piping hot.
Time: Preparation takes about 25 minutes and cooking takes about 20 minutes.

She-crab Soup

This wonderful soup gets its distinctive flavor from the crab eggs. If you are unable to obtain female crabs, crumble the yolk of hard-cooked eggs into the bottom of the soup plates before serving,

SERVES 4-6

1 Tbsp butter

1 tsp all-purpose flour

1 quart milk

2 cups white crab meat and crab eggs

½ tsp Worcestershire sauce

½ tsp mace

Few drops onion juice

½ tsp salt

⅓ tsp pepper

To serve

4 Tbsps dry sherry, warmed

¼ pint cream, whipped

Paprika or finely chopped fresh parsley

In the top of a large double boiler, melt the butter and blend in the flour until smooth. Add the milk gradually, stirring constantly. Add the crab meat and eggs and all of the seasonings. Cook the soup slowly for 20 minutes over hot water. To serve, place one tablespoon of warmed sherry into individual soup bowls, add the soup and top with whipped cream. Sprinkle with paprika or finely chopped parsley.
Time: Preparation takes 10 minutes and cooking takes 25 minutes.

Cioppino

California's famous and delicious fish stew is Italian in heritage; but a close relative of French Bouillabaisse, too.

SERVES 6-8

1 pound spinach, well washed
1 Tbsp each chopped fresh basil, thyme, rosemary, and sage
2 Tbsps chopped fresh marjoram
4 Tbsps chopped fresh parsley
1 large red bell pepper, finely chopped
2 cloves garlic, finely chopped
24 large fresh clams or 48 mussels, well scrubbed
1 large crab, cracked, or 8oz crab meat
1 pound monkfish
12 large shrimp, cooked and unpeeled
1 pound canned plum tomatoes and juice
2 Tbsps tomato paste
4 Tbsps olive oil
Salt and pepper
½-1 cup dry white wine
Water

Chop the spinach leaves coarsely after removing any tough stems. Combine the spinach with the herbs, chopped bell pepper, and garlic, and set aside.

Discard any clams or mussels with broken shells or ones that do not close when tapped. Place the shellfish in the bottom of a large pan and sprinkle over a layer of the spinach mixture. To prepare the crab, break off the claws and set them aside. Turn the crab over and press up with the thumbs to separate the body from the shell. Cut the body into quarters and use a skewer to pick out the white meat. Discard the stomach sac and the lungs. Scrape out the brown meat from the shell to use, if desired. Crack the large claws and legs and remove the meat. Break the meat into shreds, discarding any shell or cartilage. Combine the white and dark meat. Place the meat on top of the spinach and then add another spinach layer.

Add the fish and a spinach layer, followed by the shrimp and any remaining spinach. Mix the tomatoes, tomato paste, oil, wine, and seasonings and pour over the seafood and spinach. Cover the pan and simmer the mixture for about 40 minutes. If more liquid is needed, add water. Spoon into soup bowls, dividing the fish and shellfish evenly.

Time: Preparation takes about 40 minutes and cooking takes 40 minutes.

Preparation: This soup must be eaten immediately after cooking. It does not keep or reheat well.

Maine Lobster Stew

This is probably the most luxurious of the famous shellfish soup-stews from the East Coast.

SERVES 8-10

4 quarts whole milk

¼ cup heavy cream

¼ cup melted butter

1½ tsps paprika

3¼ pounds Maine lobster meat

Salt

Oyster crackers, dill pickles, and hot rolls to serve

Heat the milk and heavy cream in a double boiler. Do not allow to boil. In a heavy skillet (preferably cast iron), slowly heat the melted butter and paprika, mixing them together to create a red butter sauce. Add the cold Maine lobster and heat slowly, turning the meat until warm, but do not over-heat. Add the warmed lobster meat to the hot milk and heat gently for 1 hour. Add a pinch of salt if necessary. For best results, remove the lobster stew from the heat and refrigerate overnight. Reheat the next day. Serve with oyster crackers, dill pickles, and hot rolls.

Time: Preparation takes 30 minutes and cooking takes 1 hour.

Crawfish Etouffée

This Cajun specialty is a thick peppery stew that is served with rice. Other shellfish, such as shrimp, can also be used.

SERVES 4

⅓ cup butter or margarine

1 small onion, chopped

1 pound crawfish

6 Tbsps all-purpose flour

1 cup water or fish broth

1 Tbsp tomato paste

1 Tbsp chopped fresh parsley

2 tsps chopped fresh dill

2 tsps Tabasco sauce

Salt and pepper

Cooked rice, to serve

Melt half the butter or margarine in a saucepan, add the onion and cook to soften slightly. Add crawfish and cook quickly until it curls. Remove to a plate. Add the flour to the pan and cook slowly until golden brown, stirring frequently. Pour on the water and stir vigorously to blend. Add tomato paste and bring to a boil. Add parsley, dill, Tabasco sauce, salt, and plenty of pepper, and return the onions and crawfish to the sauce. Heat through for 5 minutes and serve over hot rice.

Time: Preparation takes 20 minutes and cooking takes 15 minutes.

Smoked Salmon Bisque

Save the salmon skin and trimmings from another recipe to make this sophisticated soup.

SERVES 6-8

Skin and trimmings of a side of smoked salmon

1 onion, stuck with cloves

1 carrot

1-2 stalks celery

Bay leaf

1 tsp salt

A few peppercorns

¼ cup butter

½ cup all-purpose flour

1 Tbsp tomato paste

1 glass white wine

4 Tbsps cream

1 Tbsp fresh parsley

P ut the skin and trimmings in a saucepan. Cut the carrot and celery into chunks. Pierce the onion with 5-6 cloves. Add these to the pan. Cover with cold water, add the bay leaf, salt, and peppercorns. Cover the pan and simmer for about 30 minutes. Remove the bay leaf. Take out the onion, remove the cloves and return the onion to the pan. With a slotted spoon, remove the fish skin and scrape off any remaining flesh, which should also be returned to the pan. Strain half the liquid into a bowl.

In another large pan melt the butter, and stir in the flour to make a roux. Stir in the tomato paste and gradually add the strained broth, stirring constantly until it thickens. Add the white wine. Put the rest of the broth, containing the fish and vegetables, in the liquidizer and run it for half a minute. Add this to the soup. Test for seasoning. Stir a spoonful of cream into the soup before serving or put a spoon of cream on top of each bowl. Garnish with a little chopped parsley.

Time: Preparation takes 30 minutes and cooking takes 1 hour.

Clam Chowder

The chowder owes its name to the French fisherman who would celebrate the safe return of the fleet by cooking fish soup on the docks in huge kettles or *chaudières*.

SERVES 6-8

2 pounds clams (or 1 pound shelled or canned clams)
All-purpose flour
3 oz rindless bacon, diced
2 medium onions, finely diced
1 Tbsp all-purpose flour
6 medium potatoes, peeled and cubed
Salt and pepper
4 cups milk
1 cup light cream
Chopped fresh parsley (optional)

Scrub the clams well and place them in a basin of cold water with a handful of flour to soak for 30 minutes. Drain the clams and place them in a deep saucepan with about ½ cup cold water. Cover and bring to a boil, stirring occasionally until all the shells open. Discard any that do not open. Strain the clam liquid, reserve it and set the clams aside to cool.

Place the diced bacon in a large, deep saucepan and cook slowly until the fat is rendered. Turn up the heat and brown the bacon. Remove it to a paper towel to drain. Add the onions to the bacon fat in the pan and cook slowly to soften. Stir in the flour and add the potatoes, salt, pepper, milk, and reserved

clam juice. Cover, bring to a boil and cook for about 10 minutes, or until the potatoes are nearly tender. Remove the clams from their shells and chop them if large. Add to the soup along with the cream and diced bacon. Cook for a further 10 minutes, or until the potatoes and clams are tender. Add the chopped parsley, if desired, and serve immediately.

Time: Preparation takes 30 minutes and cooking takes 20 minutes.

Matelote

Fresh crusty bread is all that is needed to accompany this dish.

SERVES 4

1 pound sole, cleaned

1 pound monkfish

1 small wing of skate

1 quart mussels

8 oz unpeeled shrimp

3 onions

6 Tbsps butter

1²/₃ cups dry cider or white wine

¼ cup all-purpose flour

2 Tbsps chopped fresh parsley

Salt and pepper

Lemon juice

Fillet and skin the sole. Cut the fillets into large pieces. Cut the monkfish similarly. Chop the wing of skate into 4 large pieces. Peel the shrimp and set aside. Scrub the mussels well, discarding any with broken shells. Chop the onion finely and soften in half the butter. Add the mussels and about 3-4 tablespoons water. Cover the pan and shake over a high heat until all the mussels have opened, discarding any that have not. Strain the liquid into a bowl, allow mussels to cool, then shell them. Put the cooking liquid back into a pan. Add the wine or cider, and the pieces of fish so that they are barely covered by the liquid. Simmer gently for about 8 minutes or until fish is just cooked. Mix the flour with remaining butter to a paste. Remove the cooked fish from liquid and put into a serving dish to keep warm. Bring liquid back to a boil.

Add the flour and butter paste, a little at a time, whisking it in and allowing the liquid to boil after each addition, until liquid is thickened. Add parsley, shelled shrimp, shelled mussels, a little lemon juice, and seasoning. Heat for a few minutes to warm shellfish through. Pour over fish in serving dish and sprinkle with more chopped parsley.

Time: Preparation takes 20 minutes and cooking takes 20 minutes.

Oyster Bisque

This is the perfect way to introduce newcomers to the flavor of oysters.

SERVES 4

3 dozen oysters, cleaned and shelled
²/₃ cup dry white wine
2 cups water
2 Tbsps butter
2½ Tbsps all-purpose flour
1¼ cups heavy cream
Salt, white pepper and paprika
Squeeze of lemon juice

Chop the oysters coarsely, reserving 4 for garnish. Put chopped oysters and their liquid into a medium saucepan with the water and wine. Bring to a boil and allow to simmer for 15 minutes. Blend, and measure the amount of liquid. Reduce, or add water, to make 1 pint. Melt 1½ tablespoons butter in a saucepan and when foaming, remove from heat and add flour. Cook the flour and butter together for about 1 minute until very pale brown. Add the oyster liquid gradually.

Stir well, bring back to a boil and simmer gently for about 10 minutes. Season with salt, a pinch of paprika, and a good pinch of white pepper. Add heavy cream, return to heat and boil for 1-2 minutes. Add lemon juice, if desired. Cook reserved oysters quickly in remaining butter. Put soup into warm serving dishes. Top each with 1 oyster and a sprinkling of paprika.
Time: Preparation takes 10 minutes and cooking takes about 25 minutes.

Boatman's Stew

Mushrooms add a nice contrast of texture in this fish stew.

SERVES 4-6

6 Tbsps olive oil
2 large onions, sliced
1 red bell pepper, sliced
¼ pound mushrooms, sliced
1 pound canned tomatoes
Pinch of dried thyme
Salt and pepper
1½ cups water
2 pounds whitefish fillets, skinned
½ cup white wine
2 Tbsps chopped fresh parsley

Heat the oil in a large saucepan and add the onions. Cook until beginning to look transluscent. Add the bell pepper and cook until the vegetables have softened. Add the mushrooms and the tomatoes and bring the mixture to a boil. Add the thyme, salt, pepper, and water and simmer for about 30 minutes. Add the fish and wine and cook until the fish flakes easily, about 15 minutes. Stir in the parsley.
Time: Preparation takes 20 minutes and cooking takes 45 minutes.
Variation: Shellfish may be added with the fish, if desired.
Serving Idea: Serve the stew over rice and accompany with a green salad.

Seafood Gumbo

Recipes for gumbo abound, the secret is to try one and adapt it to your own taste.

SERVES 10

2 pounds shrimp, peeled
(reserve shells to make shellfish broth)
1½ cups oil
2 cups all-purpose flour
2 cups chopped onions
1 cup chopped celery
¾ cup chopped bell pepper
¼ cup chopped garlic
2 cups green onions, sliced
1 pound smoked sausage, diced
1 pound crab meat
1 gallon shellfish stock
2 dozen oysters, shelled
Liquor from the oysters
¼ cup fresh parsley, chopped
¼ Tbsp filé powder
Salt and cayenne pepper

To make the shellfish broth, follow the recipe for fish broth on page 32, substituting the shrimp shells for the fish bones. Reserve the broth. Add the oil to a heavy-bottomed stock pot and heat over low heat. When the oil is hot, add the flour and stir constantly until a light brown roux is achieved. Add the onions, sauté for 2 minutes then add the celery, bell pepper, garlic, and the white part of the green onions. Cook for 2 minutes, stirring constantly. Add the sausage and blend well into the roux. Stir in the crab meat and 1 pound of the shrimp. Blend well into the roux until the shrimp begin to turn pink. Add the broth, 1 ladle at a time, blending after each addition until it is well incorporated. Continue adding broth until the gumbo achieves a soup-like texture. Simmer for 35 minutes, adding remaining stock to retain the volume. Add half of the onion tops, the oyster liquor, remaining shrimp, and parsley. Cook for 5 minutes then add the oysters, remaining onion, and filé powder. Remove the gumbo from the heat, and allow to stand for 15 minutes, or until thickened. Season to taste with salt and cayenne pepper.
Time: Preparation takes 45 minutes and cooking takes 50 minutes.

Coconut Shrimp Soup

Soup is usually served as part of a full Thai meal, but is also served at any time as a snack.

SERVES 4

1 stem of lemon grass
8 oz jumbo shrimp
1 quart fish broth
4 slices galangal
4 kaffir lime leaves, shredded
2 red or green chilies, chopped
1 Tbsp fish sauce
8 oz skinned whitefish fillets, cut into strips
⅔ cup thick coconut milk

Thinly slice a piece of the lemon grass about 2 inches long. Peel the jumbo shrimp leaving just the tails. Pull away the dark vein from the shrimp and discard. Heat the broth in a large saucepan until almost boiling and stir in the galangal, lime leaves, lemon grass, chilies, and fish sauce. Simmer for 2 minutes. Add the fish strips and shrimp and cook gently for 5 minutes, or until the fish looks opaque. Stir in the coconut milk and continue cooking until very hot, but do not allow to boil.

Time: Preparation takes 20 minutes and cooking takes 10 minutes.
Cook's Tip: Use a firm-fleshed fish that won't break up too much during cooking.
Variation: Ginger can be used instead of galangal.

Crab & Watercress Soup

Crab and watercress make a great combination in this quick soup.

SERVES 4-6

6 cups chicken broth
4 oz white crab meat, shredded
2 green onions, finely chopped
2 bunches watercress, finely chopped
Salt and pepper
1 tsp cornstarch
1 Tbsp water
2 tsps light soy sauce
A few drops sesame oil

Bring the broth to a boil with the crab meat, onions and watercress and simmer for 4-5 minutes. Add salt and pepper to taste.

Mix the cornstarch with the water and add to the soup. Allow to simmer for a further 2 minutes. Add soy sauce and sesame oil, mix well and simmer for 2 minutes. Serve immediately.

Time: Preparation takes 10 minutes and cooking takes 8-9 minutes.
Cook's Tip: Ensure the watercress is not limp – it deteriorates rapidly once it reaches the supermarket.

Seafood Stew

Clams are crucial to this stew so buy the freshest you can find.

SERVES 6

24 clams in the shell

3 squid, cleaned and cut into rings

2 pounds firm whitefish, filleted into 2-inch pieces

3 medium tomatoes, peeled, seeded, and chopped

1/2 green bell pepper, chopped

1 small onion, chopped

1 clove garlic, finely chopped

1 cup dry white wine

Salt and pepper

1/2 cup olive oil

6 slices French bread

3 Tbsps chopped fresh parsley

Scrub the clams well to remove any barnacles. Discard any with broken shells or ones that do not close when tapped. Place the clams in a large saucepan, scatter over them about half of the vegetables and garlic and spoon over 4 tablespoons of the olive oil.

Scatter the squid and the prepared whitefish over the vegetables in the pan and top with the remaining vegetables. Pour in the white wine and season with salt and pepper. Bring to a boil over high heat and then reduce to simmering. Cover the pan and cook for about 20 minutes or until the clams open, the squid is tender, and the fish flakes easily. Discard any clams that do not open. Heat the remaining olive oil in a skillet and when hot, add the slices of bread, browning them well on both sides. Drain on paper towels. Place a slice of bread in the bottom of a soup bowl and ladle the fish mixture over the bread. Sprinkle with parsley and serve immediately.

Time: Preparation takes 35 minutes and cooking takes 20 minutes.

Light Meals

Given our current appetite for light, healthful meals it is hardly surprising that our tastes seem to be moving away from the meaty soul-satisfying food that was once at the heart of American meals. As meat moves down the menu, so lighter sources of protein, such as seafood, move up. More than ever we are now eating meals that past generations would have considered snack food and certainly not a satisfactory meal to end the day on. This is perhaps also due to the fact we have tended to restructure our eating habits to eat more earlier in the day rather than filling up in the evening.

In the past, seafood was often reserved for special meals rather than being seen as an everyday food, but this finally seems to be changing as America's cooks realize the full value of the oceans' bounty. No longer simply reserved for special occasions, seafood now finds its way into numerous meals.

Light meals are all about enjoyable, carefree eating and whether you are looking for something for a simple lunch for friends or a light evening meal for the family, you will find the perfect recipe in this chapter. Most of the recipes are reasonably quick, although this does not mean they are ordinary. Omelet of Clams and Mussels, for instance, is the ultimate recipe for the cook who wants to provide something unusual that is stunningly simple – serve with a green salad and some crusty fresh bread and you have the perfect answer. If, on the other hand, you want to impress with something that takes a little more time but is nonetheless light on the stomach, try Crab and Spinach Roulade; it's healthy, delicious, and it looks great too.

The lasting popularity of Chinese food is understandable considering America's growing love affair with healthly food. The majority of Chinese stir-fry recipes offer the cook the ultimate in adaptability, speed, and convenience, and for light meals nothing could be better. We feature a number of delicious Chinese seafood recipes, such as Shrimp with Snow Peas, that can be prepared in no time at all and, as with most stir-fry recipes, they can be easily adapted to a different number of guests. Italy is another source of inspiration in this chapter. Pasta seems to rule supreme and its popularity shows little sign of abating. Perhaps the only thing that has changed is that we have moved away from the heavy pasta bakes that were once so prevalent in America's kitchens to a preference for dishes that are not quite so demanding on the digestive system! With this in mind we have included two delightfully appetizing light meals – Pasta with Leeks and Mussels, and Fettuccine with Smoked Salmon – that appeal to the taste buds without overloading the system.

With everything from an omelet to a roulade this chapter has a recipe for every occasion, so don't feel that simply because the recipes are labelled "light" that they are somehow not good enough for a special occasion; with the addition of a few side dishes or another course, many are good enough to grace the most elegant table.

Shrimp Risotto

Use medium-sized shrimp that come about 25 to the pound for this recipe.

SERVES 4

1 pound unpeeled shrimp

1 glass white wine

4 fresh tomatoes

3 cloves garlic

1 large onion

3 Tbsps olive oil

2 Tbsps chopped fresh parsley

1 cup brown rice

1 tsp tomato paste

Salt and pepper

2 Tbsps grated Parmesan cheese

Peel the shrimp, leaving 4 unpeeled for a garnish. Put the shrimp shells and the wine into a saucepan and bring to a boil. Remove the pan from the heat and allow to cool completely before straining out the shrimp shells. Reserve the liquid. Chop the tomatoes coarsely and remove the cores. Peel and chop the garlic and onion. Heat the olive oil in a large skillet. Cook the onion and garlic gently in the oil, without browning them. Stir in the parsley and cook for about 30 seconds. Add the rice to the fried onion, and stir well to coat the grains with the oil. Add the wine, tomato paste, tomatoes, and just enough cold water to cover the rice. Season the rice with salt and pepper, and cook for about 20 minutes, until all the water is absorbed and the rice is tender. When the rice is cooked, stir in the peeled shrimp and the cheese. Heat through gently, place in a serving dish and top with the unpeeled shrimp.

Time: Preparation takes 15 minutes and cooking takes 25 minutes.

Grilled Fish

Grilling fish with herbs and lemon is one of the most
delightful ways of preparing it, and is particularly
common in the Greek Islands.

SERVES 4

2 large bream or other whole fish

Fresh thyme and oregano

Olive oil

Lemon juice

Salt and pepper

Lemon wedges

Vine leaves

Preheat a broiler. Clean the fish and rinse it well. Pat dry and
sprinkle the cavity with salt, pepper, and lemon juice. Place sprigs
of herbs inside. Make 3 diagonal cuts on the sides of the fish with a
sharp knife. Place the fish on the broiler rack and sprinkle with olive
oil and lemon juice. Cook on both sides until golden brown and crisp.
This should take about 8-10 minutes per side, depending on the
thickness of the fish. If using vine leaves preserved in brine, rinse
them well. If using fresh vine leaves, pour over boiling water and leave
to stand for about 10 minutes to soften slightly. Drain and allow to
cool. Line a large serving platter with the vine leaves and when the
fish is cooked place it on top of the leaves. Serve surrounded with
lemon wedges.

Time: Preparation takes 20 minutes and cooking takes 16-20 minutes.

Cook's Tip: When broiling large whole fish, slit the skin on both sides
to help the fish cook evenly.

Variation: The fish may be wrapped in vine leaves before broiling.
This keeps the fish moist and adds extra flavor.

Boiled Maine Lobster

With today's lobster prices, it's hard to imagine that
American colonists considered this delectable seafood
humble and ordinary.

SERVES 4

Water

Salt or seaweed

4 1-pound live lobsters

Lemon wedges

Fresh parsley sprigs to garnish

1 cup butter, melted

Fill a large stock pot with water and add salt or a piece of
seaweed. Bring the water to a boil and then turn off the heat.
Place the live lobsters into the pot, keeping your hand well away
from the claws. Lower them in claws first. Bring the water slowly
back to a boil and cook the lobsters for about 15 minutes, or until
they turn bright red. Remove them from the water and drain
briefly on paper towels. Place on a plate and garnish the plate with
lemon wedges and parsley sprigs. Serve with individual dishes of
melted butter for dipping.

Time: Preparation takes 5 minutes and cooking takes 15 minutes.

Pasta with Leeks & — Mussels —

This rather unusual pasta dish is surprisingly easy to prepare.

SERVES 6

3 cups mussels
½ cup white wine
1 shallot, chopped
2 medium leeks
¾ cup heavy cream
1 pound spiral-shaped pasta
1 Tbsp oil
2 slices ham
1½ Tbsps butter
Chopped chives to garnish
Salt and pepper

Scrub the mussels, remove the beards, and wash in several changes of water to eliminate the sand. In a large, covered saucepan, cook the mussels in the white wine with the chopped shallot for approximately 5 minutes, over a high heat, until the mussels open. Cool, and remove the mussels from their shells. Reserve the cooking liquid.

Quarter each leek lengthwise, wash thoroughly, and slice finely. In a covered saucepan, cook the leeks in the cream, with salt and pepper to taste, for 10 minutes over a low heat. Boil the pasta with 1 tablespoon oil.

Stir the pasta occasionally as it cooks, to prevent sticking. Drain after 5 or 6 minutes. Rinse in cold water to prevent sticking. Remove any fat or rind from the ham, and slice into small pieces. Strain the mussel cooking liquid through a sieve lined with muslin. Measure out approximately ½ cup. Add the shelled mussels and the mussel liquid to the cream mixture and cook for 4 minutes, stirring constantly. Melt the butter in a deep skillet and reheat the pasta gently with the ham. Season to taste. When the pasta is heated through, add the cream and leek sauce, and serve garnished with the chopped chives.

Time: Preparation takes 30 minutes, cooking takes 25 minutes.

Cook's Tip: Use your favorite kind of ham in this dish.

Lobster a la Crème

Be careful not to overdo the sherry in this recipe as it will overpower the flavor of the lobster.

SERVES 4

1 cold, boiled lobster

1¼ cups heavy cream

4 Tbsps butter

¼ cup dry sherry or Madeira

Squeeze of lemon juice

Ground nutmeg

3 Tbsps dry bread crumbs

1 small bunch of fresh tarragon, chopped

Salt and pepper

Cut lobster in half lengthwise with a sharp knife. Remove meat from tail. Crack claws and remove meat. Remove as much meat as possible from the legs. Chop all the meat coarsely. Melt 3 tablespoons of the butter in a sauté pan and sauté the lobster with the seasonings, lemon juice, nutmeg, and tarragon. Flame the sherry or Madeira and pour over the lobster in the sauté pan until flames die out. Pour over the heavy cream and bring to a boil. Allow to boil for 5 minutes until cream begins to thicken.

Spoon into individual serving dishes. Melt remaining butter in a small skillet and brown the dry bread crumbs. When golden brown and crisp, sprinkle over the top of the lobster.

Time: Preparation takes 10 minutes and cooking takes 5 minutes.

Steamed Clams

This simple way to use clams brings out all their flavor.

SERVES 1

7-8 medium sized soft-shell clams (steamers), scrubbed

¼ cup water

½-1 cup butter, melted

Place the clams in a medium-sized kettle with the water. Cover and cook on medium heat until the clam juice boils up through the clams and all the clams have opened. Discard any that do not open. Serve them hot with melted butter and the clam broth. To eat, remove the tissue from the neck, dip the clam in the broth and then into the butter.

Time: Preparation takes 15 minutes and cooking takes 10 minutes.

Cook's Tip: Soak the clams in a basin of cold water with a handful of flour for about 30 minutes. This plumps them up and also helps them eliminate sand and grit.

Sole Surprise

This recipe consists of little puff paste "boxes" filled with spinach, with the fillets of sole laid on top and coated with a cheese sauce.

SERVES 4

8 oz frozen puff paste
8 oz frozen spinach
¼ cup butter
4 small or 2 large fillets of sole

Sauce

2 Tbsps butter
2 Tbsps all-purpose flour
1¼ cups milk
Pinch of fennel
Salt and pepper
½ cup grated cheese

Roll out the defrosted pastry into a rectangle 5x8 inches. Cut into four equal size rectangles 2½x4 inches. Follow the same procedure for each one. Fold the pastry over, short sides together. Cut out the center with a sharp knife, leaving ½ inch all round. Roll out the center piece on a floured board until it is the same size as the ½ inch "frame". Brush the edges with milk and put the "frame" on the base. Brush the top with milk and place on a greased cookie sheet. Bake the pastry in a preheated 425°F oven for 10-15 minutes.

Meanwhile, put the spinach in a pan with ¼ inch water and a little salt. Cover and cook for 4-5 minutes. Drain and beat in half the butter. Skin the fillets and, if necessary, cut them in two. Use the rest of the butter to coat two plates and put the fillets on one and cover them with the other. Cook them over a pan of boiling water for 20 minutes, or until the flesh looks opaque and flakes easily.

For the sauce, melt the 2 tablespoons butter with the flour to make a roux. Gradually stir in the milk. Bring to a boil. Reduce heat and add fennel and salt and pepper; cook for another minute or two. Remove from the heat and stir in the grated cheese. Divide the spinach between the four pastry boxes. Lay the sole on top and top the fish with the cheese sauce.

Time: Preparation takes 30 minutes and cooking takes 30 minutes.

Plaice & Mushroom — Turnovers —

These delicious individual pies make a warming family lunch or supper dish.

SERVES 4

4 plaice fillets, skinned
Salt and pepper
Scant ½ cup milk
1 cup button mushrooms, trimmed and thinly sliced
2 Tbsps butter
Juice 1 lemon
3 Tbsps hazelnut or lemon stuffing mix
12 oz puff paste
Beaten egg, for glazing
Poppy seeds, for sprinkling

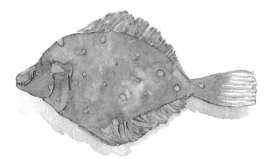

Season the plaice fillets and roll them up jelly roll fashion. Secure each roll with a wooden pick and poach gently in the milk in a preheated 350°F oven for about 10 minutes, or until the flesh looks opaque. Drain the fish and allow it to cool. Remove the wooden picks. Increase the oven temperature to 400°F.

Put the mushrooms and butter into a pan with the lemon juice. Cook over a moderate heat for about 5 minutes. Allow the mushrooms to cool and then stir in the stuffing mix. Roll out the paste, quite thinly, into 4 circles, each 6 inches in diameter. Brush the edges with beaten egg. Put a fish roll into the center of each paste circle and top with a quarter of the mushroom mixture. Pull the paste edges up and over the fish and pinch together to seal. Place the turnovers on a greased cookie sheet and glaze with the beaten egg. Sprinkle with a few poppy seeds. Bake in the reset oven for about 25 minutes, or until well risen, puffed, and golden. Serve piping hot.

Time: Preparation will take 25 minutes, plus the cooling time. Cooking takes about 35 minutes.

Variation: Make these turnovers with whole-wheat puff paste for an even more nutritious dish.

Fettuccine with Salmon & Caviar

This is the perfect way to impress your guests and you need only small amounts of the more expensive ingredients.

SERVES 4

½ pound green fettuccine

2 Tbsps butter or margarine

Juice of half a lemon

Pepper

¼ pound smoked salmon, cut into strips

2 Tbsps heavy cream

2 Tbsps red caviar or lumpfish roe

Garnish

8 lemon slices

Cook the fettuccine in lots of boiling, salted water for 10 minutes, or until tender but still firm. Rinse under hot water, and drain well. Heat the butter in a pan and add lemon juice and freshly ground black pepper. Add fettuccine to pan, and then add smoked salmon. Toss together. Serve topped with heavy cream and a sprinkling of red caviar. Garnish with lemon slices and serve immediately.

Time: Preparation takes 5 minutes and cooking takes 15 minutes.

Cook's Tip: Ensure the fettuccine is well drained otherwise it will water down the butter sauce.

Shrimp with Snow Peas

Snow peas are perfectly suited to stir-frying, as are shrimp.

SERVES 2-4

3 Tbsps oil

½ cup split blanched almonds, halved

4 oz snow peas

2 oz bamboo shoots, sliced

2 tsps cornstarch

2 tsps light soy sauce

¾ cup chicken broth

2 Tbsps dry sherry

Salt and pepper

1 pound cooked, peeled shrimp

Heat the oil in a wok. Add the almonds and cook over moderate heat until golden brown. Remove from the oil and drain on paper towels.

To prepare the snow peas, tear off the stems and pull them downwards to remove any strings. If the snow peas are small, just remove the stalks. Add the snow peas to the hot oil and cook for about 1 minute. Remove and set aside with the almonds. Drain all the oil from the wok and mix together the cornstarch and the remaining ingredients, except the shrimp and bamboo shoots. Pour the mixture into the wok and stir constantly while bringing to a boil. Allow to simmer for 1-2 minutes until thickened. Stir in the shrimp and all the other ingredients and heat through for about 1 minute. Serve immediately.

Time: Preparation takes about 10 minutes and cooking takes 6-8 minutes.

Soufflés St. Jacques

Try this recipe during the winter months and early spring when the scallops have large roes.

SERVES 4

8 large or 16 small scallops, with roe attached (if possible)

1¼ cups milk

2½ Tbsps butter

2½ Tbsps all-purpose flour

2½ Tbsps grated cheddar cheese

4 eggs

Salt and pepper

¼ tsp Dijon mustard

Tomato sauce

1¼ cups canned tomatoes

1 small onion, finely chopped

Bay leaf

Pinch of thyme

Sugar

Half a clove of garlic, finely chopped

1 Tbsp Worcestershire sauce

Salt and pepper

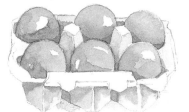

First prepare the tomato sauce. Combine the onion with the rest of the ingredients in a small, heavy saucepan. Bring to a boil, then lower heat, leaving to simmer, half-covered, for 20 minutes. Strain the sauce and set aside. Poach the scallops in milk for about 5 minutes. Remove from milk and set aside. Melt the butter in a small saucepan and, when foaming, remove from heat and stir in flour. Add milk in which scallops were poached. Bring to a boil, stirring constantly until thickened. Add salt and pepper, then stir in the grated cheese. Leave to cool slightly. Separate eggs, beat the yolks and add them to the cheese sauce. Butter 4 deep scallop shells or porcelain baking dishes. Slice scallops through the middle, horizontally. Reserve 1 whole roe per serving. Place scallops in bottom of the shells. Beat the egg whites until stiff but not dry, and fold into cheese mixture.

Divide soufflé mixture between the scallop shells, and place them on a cookie sheet. Bake in a preheated 450°F oven for about 10 minutes or until well risen and lightly browned. Meanwhile, reheat tomato sauce and spoon some of it, when scallops are ready, into each dish. Serve remaining tomato sauce separately. Garnish each serving with the reserved whole roe.
Time: Preparation takes 20 minutes and cooking takes 20 minutes.

Fish & Zucchini
— Kebabs —

These kebabs are ideal served on a bed of brown rice, sprinkled with parsley.

SERVES 4

16 small, thin sole fillets, or 8 larger ones, skinned and cut in half lengthwise
4 Tbsps olive oil
1 clove garlic, finely chopped
Juice of ½ lemon
Finely grated rind ½ lemon
Salt and pepper
3 drops Tabasco sauce
2 medium zucchini, cut into ¼-inch slices
1 green bell pepper, cut into 1-inch pieces

Roll up each sole fillet like a jelly roll and secure with a wooden pick. Place the fish rolls in a shallow dish. Mix together the olive oil, garlic, lemon juice, lemon rind, salt and pepper, and Tabasco sauce. Spoon the olive oil mixture evenly over the fish rolls, and chill for about 2 hours.

Remove the wooden picks, and carefully thread the rolled fish fillets onto kebab skewers alternately with the zucchini slices and pieces of bell pepper. Brush each threaded kebab with a little of the lemon and oil marinade. Arrange the kebab skewers on a broiler pan and cook under a moderately hot broiler for about 8 minutes or until lightly browned, carefully turning the kebabs once or twice during cooking and brushing them with a little of the remaining marinade.

Time: Preparation takes about 30 minutes, plus 2 hours chilling time, and cooking takes about 8 minutes.

Cook's Tip: The marinade ingredients are delicious used with other types of fish.

Jekyll Island Shrimp

Named for an island off the Georgia coast, this makes an elegant light lunch.

SERVES 2

2 pounds cooked shrimp

4 Tbsps butter, softened

Pinch of salt, white pepper, and cayenne pepper

1 clove garlic, finely chopped

6 Tbsps fine dry bread crumbs

2 Tbsps chopped fresh parsley

4 Tbsps sherry

Lemon wedges or slices

To prepare the shrimp, remove the heads and legs first. Peel off the shells, carefully removing the tail shells. Arrange shrimp in a shallow casserole or individual dishes.

Combine the remaining ingredients, except the lemon garnish, mixing well. Spread the mixture to completely cover the shrimp and place in a preheated 375°F oven for about 20 minutes, or until the butter melts and the crumbs become crisp. Garnish with lemon wedges or slices.

Time: Preparation takes 35-40 minutes and cooking takes 20 minutes.

Cook's Tip: Try to use fresh cooked shrimp, frozen shrimp will not have quite the same flavor.

Omelet of Clams — & Mussels —

If you are entertaining, make a small individual omelet for each of your guests.

SERVES 4

½ pint shelled clams

½ pint shelled mussels

6-8 eggs

2½ Tbsps butter

Drop of anchovy paste

Cayenne pepper

Salt and pepper

Finely chopped fresh parsley and chives

Poach the mussels in boiling, salted water for about 2 minutes. Add a bay leaf if desired. Rinse the clams under cold water. Separate the eggs and beat the yolks with the anchovy paste, cayenne pepper, and seasoning. Whisk the whites until stiff but not dry and fold into yolks. Heat the butter in a large omelet pan and when foaming, pour in the egg mixture. Allow the eggs to set on the bottom. Score the omelet down the middle. Add clams and mussels and fold in two. Heat through for 2 minutes to cook the inside of the omelet and to warm the shellfish. Serve immediately, sprinkled with the chopped parsley and chives.

Time: Preparation takes 5 minutes and cooking takes about 8 minutes.

Cook's Tip: If you find clams difficult to get, substitute more mussels.

Mussels à la Greque

Fresh mussels are a real treat during the fall and winter, and the sauce in this recipe is a reminder of warmer days!

SERVES 4

4 cups mussels

1 onion, chopped

½ cup white wine

Lemon juice

2 Tbsps olive oil

1 clove garlic, finely chopped

1 shallot or 2 green onions, chopped

1½ pounds fresh tomatoes, chopped

1 tsp fennel seeds

1 tsp coriander seeds

1 tsp oregano

1 bay leaf

1 Tbsp chopped fresh basil

Pinch of cayenne pepper

Salt and pepper

Black olives, to garnish

Scrub the mussels and discard any with broken shells, or which do not shut when tapped with a knife. Put them into a large saucepan with the onion, wine, and lemon juice. Cover and cook quickly until the mussels open, discarding any that do not. Remove the mussels from their shells and leave to cool. Reserve the cooking liquid.

Heat the olive oil in a saucepan and add the garlic and the shallot or green onions. Cook gently until golden brown. Stir in the tomatoes, spices, and herbs. Season to taste and blend in the reserved liquor from the mussels. Bring this mixture to a boil and allow to boil rapidly until the tomatoes are soft and the liquid is reduced by half. Remove the bay leaf. Allow the sauce to cool, then stir in the mussels. Chill well and serve garnished with black olives.

Time: Preparation takes about 20 minutes and cooking takes about 20 minutes.

Preparation: The shells of fresh mussels must be tightly closed and intact. Any that are cracked or do not shut tight when tapped with a knife should be thrown away. Any mussels that remain closed after being cooked, should also be discarded.

Seafood with Egg Noodles

Use any mixture of seafood in this spicy dish.

SERVES 4

1 pound mixed seafood, such as shrimp, chunks of fish,
squid, clams, and mussels

3 large green chilies, seeded and chopped

1 Tbsp chopped fresh coriander leaves

2 cloves garlic, finely chopped

6 oz egg noodles

2 Tbsps oil

4 oz snow peas

4 oz baby corn cobs

½ red bell pepper, sliced

1 Tbsp fish sauce

⅔ cup fish broth

1 Tbsp lime juice

2 tsps cornstarch

Cook the seafood separately in boiling water until cooked through, then drain and set aside. If using squid, score the hoods in a diamond pattern before cutting into pieces.

Pound the chilies, coriander, and garlic together in a pestle and mortar. Cook the noodles as directed on the packet. Heat the oil in a wok, add the baby corn, snow peas, and pepper and stir-fry for 4 minutes. Add the chili mixture and fish sauce and cook for 2 minutes. Stir in the fish broth and add the cooked seafood and noodles to the pan. Mix the lime juice and cornstarch together. Stir into the wok and cook until thickened.

Time: Preparation takes 15 minutes and cooking takes 15 minutes.

Cook's Tip: Scoring the squid helps to keep it tender during cooking.

Shrimp Fu Yung

This dish is perfect for lunch or an evening snack.

SERVES 4-6

Oil

1-2 cloves garlic, chopped

4 oz shrimp, peeled

4 oz green beans, sliced

1 carrot, shredded

6 eggs

Salt and pepper

1 cup chicken broth

¼ tsp salt

2 tsps soy sauce

1 tsp sugar

1 tsp cornstarch

Heat 2 tablespoons oil in a wok. Add the garlic and stir-fry for 1 minute. Add the shrimp and stir-fry for 1 minute, or until pink and curled. Add the beans and carrots and stir-fry for 2 minutes. Remove and put to one side. Beat the eggs with salt and pepper to taste, and add the cooled shrimp mixture. Clean the wok and heat 1 teaspoon oil. Pour in 4 tablespoons of the egg mixture and cook like a pancake. When the egg is set, turn the pancake over and cook on the other side until lightly golden. Keep warm while preparing the remaining pancakes.

To make the sauce, beat the broth with the salt, soy sauce, sugar, and cornstarch and stir over a gentle heat until the sauce thickens. Serve the pancakes with this sauce.

Time: Preparation takes 10 minutes and cooking takes about 20 minutes in total.

Swordfish Kebabs

Swordfish is perfect for kebabs as it is firm-fleshed and holds its shape well when cut.

SERVES 4-6

2¼ pounds swordfish steaks
6 Tbsps olive oil
1 tsp dried oregano
1 tsp dried marjoram
Juice and rind of ½ a lemon
1 pound cherry tomatoes
2 lemons, cut in thin slices
Salt and pepper
Lemon slices and fresh coriander to garnish

Cut the swordfish steaks into 2-inch pieces. Mix the olive oil, herbs, lemon juice, and rind together and set aside. Thread the swordfish, tomato slices, and lemon slices onto skewers, alternating the ingredients. Brush the skewers with the oil and lemon juice mixture and cook under a preheated broiler for about 10 minutes, or until the fish looks opaque, basting frequently. Serve garnished with lemons and coriander.

Time: Preparation takes 15 minutes and cooking takes about 10 minutes.

Oysters à la Crème

Oysters can be bought out of season but they are expensive, so try this recipe when you can buy them fresh from the fish market.

SERVES 4

2 dozen oysters on the half shell or unopened
4 Tbsps heavy cream
4 Tbsps cream cheese
1 Tbsp chopped fresh parsley
Salt and pepper
Nutmeg
Fresh coriander leaves to garnish

Scrub the oyster shells well, if unopened, and leave to soak in clean water for 2 hours. Insert an oyster knife near the hinge and pry open. Remove any pieces of broken shell from the inside and press the oysters in a circle onto a baking pan filled with rock salt. Mix together the heavy cream, cream cheese, parsley, and salt and pepper. Top each oyster with the cream mixture. Sprinkle with nutmeg and place in a preheated 350°F oven for 18-20 minutes until browned. Garnish with coriander leaves and serve immediately.

Time: Preparation takes 15 minutes and cooking takes about 20 minutes.

Crab & Spinach — Roulade —

This delicious, healthful recipe makes a perfect light luncheon.

SERVES 4

Roulade

1 pound spinach, washed

1 Tbsp butter

4 eggs, separated

Parmesan cheese, grated

Salt and pepper

Filling

½ cup crab meat

¼ cup mushrooms, thinly sliced

1 Tbsp butter

1 Tbsp all-purpose flour

⅔ cup milk

Nutmeg

2-3 Tbsps cream

Paprika

Cayenne pepper

Lemon juice

Cook the spinach in boiling salted water for about 3 minutes. Drain, rinse under cold water, and press well to remove excess liquid. Put the spinach into a food processor with the butter and egg yolks and process to a smooth purée. Whisk the egg whites until stiff but not dry and fold into the spinach. Line a 12 x 8 inch jelly roll pan with wax paper. Spread in the spinach mixture and dust with Parmesan cheese. Bake in the top half of a preheated 400°F oven for 10 minutes or until mixture has risen and is firm to the touch.

Meanwhile, prepare the filling. Sauté the sliced mushrooms in butter. Remove from heat and add flour, paprika, Cayenne, lemon juice, and seasoning to taste. Pour on the milk and bring to a boil, then simmer to a creamy consistency. Remove the pan from the heat and stir in nutmeg and cream. Stir in the crab meat. When the roulade is cooked, quickly turn it out onto a clean towel, cheese side down, and peel off the paper in which it was cooked. Spread it with the filling, roll up as for a jelly roll, starting at the short end, and serve sprinkled with more Parmesan cheese if desired.

Time: Preparation takes 15 minutes, cooking takes 15 minutes.

Mussel Risotto

To turn this risotto into a dish fit for the most sophisticated dinner party, all you need to do is press it into a round mould and then turn out and decorate with parsley.

SERVES 4

1 quart small mussels
1 pound rice
1 shallot, chopped
1/3 cup white wine
1 onion, chopped
1/4 cup butter
Saffron (powdered variety)
Salt and pepper

Clean the mussels under plenty of running water, scraping and brushing off any sand and grit. Place the clean mussels in a large saucepan with the shallot and the wine. Cook over a high heat until the mussels open. Set the saucepan aside to allow the mussels to cool. Once they are cool, remove the mussels from their shells. Strain the cooking juices through a fine sieve which has been covered with muslin. Discard all but the juice and the mussels.

Melt the butter in a skillet and gently fry the onion and the rice. Fry until the rice is transparent (approximately 1 minute) and then pour over the cooking juices made up to 3 cups with water. Stir in 2 to 3 pinches of saffron, just enough to slightly color the liquid. Transfer to an ovenproof dish, season with salt and pepper and stir in the mussels. Cover and cook in a preheated 400°F oven for approximately 20 minutes. Serve hot.
Time: Preparation takes about 10 minutes and total cooking time is 35 minutes.

Lobster Newburg

This special occasion dish is simplicity itself to prepare.

SERVES 4

1 large cooked lobster
1 1/4 cups heavy cream
2 egg yolks
2 Tbsps butter
1/4 cup dry sherry
Salt and pepper
1/4 tsp paprika
Cayenne pepper
1 tsp tomato paste

Heat the butter in a medium saucepan, add paprika and cook for 1 minute. Cut the lobster in half. Remove the tail and claws, and then the meat from these sections. Remove as much meat from the rest of the lobster as possible and add it to the pan, along with tail and claw meat.

Add the sherry and cook for 1 minute. Remove the tail and claw meat, and set aside for garnish. Mix egg yolks and cream together, and put in the pan with the lobster. Add the paprika, cayenne, tomato paste, and seasoning, and cook over a very low heat until the mixture begins to thicken. Garnish with the tail and claw meat.
Time: Preparation takes 10 minutes and cooking takes 12 minutes.
Serving Idea: Serve with buttered rice, tossed with fresh parsley.

Scallops in Saffron Sauce

Scallops are in season during fall and winter so prepare this unusual dish when they are at their freshest.

SERVES 4

16 large scallops

½ cup water

½ cup dry white wine

1 shallot, coarsely chopped

1 bouquet garni, consisting of 1 bay leaf, 1 sprig of fresh thyme
and 3 stalks of parsley

6 black peppercorns

A few strands of saffron

4 Tbsps hot water

1¼ cups heavy cream

3 Tbsps chopped fresh parsley

Salt and pepper

Put the scallops into a large shallow pan together with the water, wine, shallot, bouquet garni, and peppercorns. Cover the pan and bring the liquid almost to a boil. Remove the pan from the heat and leave the scallops to poach in the hot liquid for 10-15 minutes. The scallops are cooked when they are just firm to the touch. Remove them from the liquid and keep warm on a plate. Strain the scallop cooking liquid into a small saucepan and bring to a boil. Allow the liquid to boil rapidly until it is reduced by about half.

Soak the saffron in the hot water for about 5 minutes, or until the color has infused into the water. Add the saffron with its soaking liquid, the heavy cream and the chopped parsley to the reduced cooking liquid and season to taste. Bring the sauce to just below boiling point. Arrange the scallops on a serving plate and pour some of the sauce over them before serving. Serve the remaining sauce separately.

Time: Preparation takes 15 minutes and cooking takes about 15 minutes.

Salads & Barbecue Dishes

One of the great advances in cooking in the nineties is the recognition that the fresh flavor of ingredients is perhaps the most vital element in a successful recipe. The spectacular rise in popularity of salads is, in part, a reflection of this healthier attitude to food. Combine this with our growing love of seafood and you begin to understand why it has become such a popular salad ingredient.

Seafood is particularly appropriate for use in salads as it has a subtle flavor that does not overpower the delicate flavors of many salad ingredients. It is also quick cooking and will usually be ready by the time the other ingredients have been prepared. The suitability of seafood for salad recipes is reflected in this chapter by light, refreshing recipes such as Shrimp in Melon, and Crab and Citrus Salad, as well as heartier recipes such as Red Snapper Niçoise and Mariner's Salad. As we have stressed many times before, the emphasis is on freshness and there is nowhere that a rather out-of-date piece of fish will rear its ugly head more than in a salad, so be warned. If you get to know the people at your local fish market and use them regularly they will soon realize that you will not accept inferior produce. If you have a good supplier and you really want to impress your fish-loving guests then try the Salade aux Fruits de Mer; it is the piece de résistance of seafood dishes.

The barbecue is another growing trend that has been infiltrated by seafood. Once the preserve of burgers and ribs, the barbecue thankfully now plays host to a variety of exciting and inspiring seafood dishes. Grilling is a particularly appropriate way to cook seafood as it is quick and easy and, so long as you don't use strongly flavored coals, it does not mask its flavor but adds a subtle smoky hint. Strongly flavored oily fish, such as mackerel and sardines, are particularly good barbecue fare as their oil content keeps them moist, while their rich flavor is perfectly complemented by the rather punchy sauces often favored at barbecues.

Seafood kebabs are also becoming a great favorite and we feature three particularly delicious recipes in this chapter – Monkfish and Pepper Kebabs, Scallop and Shrimp Kebabs, and Smoked Fish Kebabs.

Grilling is one of our oldest cooking techniques and with just a little practice anyone can master the art. There are so many variable factors involved in grilling food on a barbecue that exact cooking times are not usually given and it is often down to the cook's good judgement. A good starting point is not to have the grill any closer than 4 inches from the coals – 4-6 inches is about normal. In addition, be careful of the type of coals – mesquite coals, for example, burn two to three times hotter than charcoal briquettes. Outdoor eating is great fun, so when summer comes round treat your guests to some seafood salads and barbecue dishes, you'll find it so much more interesting than the usual ribs and burgers.

Mariner's Salad

Wonderfully rich and creamy, this salad is perfect for a summer picnic.

SERVES 6

1 pound pasta shells, plain and spinach
4 large scallops, cleaned
1/2 pint frozen mussels, defrosted
1/4 pint lemon juice and water mixed
1 cup cooked shrimp, shelled
1/4 pint small clams, cooked
1 cup crab meat, cubed
4 green onions, chopped
1 Tbsp chopped fresh parsley

Dressing
Grated rind and juice of 1/2 lemon
1 1/4 cups mayonnaise
2 tsps paprika
1/3 cup sour cream or plain yogurt
Salt and pepper

Cook the pasta for 10 minutes in a large pan of boiling, salted water with 1 tablespoon oil. Drain and rinse under hot water. Leave in cold water until ready to use.

Cook the scallops and mussels in the lemon juice and water mixture for about 5 minutes, or until fairly firm. Cut the scallops into 2 or 3 pieces, depending upon size. Mix the dressing ingredients together. Drain the pasta thoroughly. Mix all ingredients together to coat completely with dressing, stirring carefully. Chill for up to 1 hour before serving.
Time: Preparation takes 25 minutes, cooking takes 15 minutes.

Salmon & Vegetable Salad

The fish in this salad "cooks" in the refrigerator in its vinegar marinade. Insist on very fresh fish for this recipe.

SERVES 4

12 oz salmon or salmon trout fillets
2 carrots, peeled and diced
1 large zucchini, diced
1 large turnip, peeled and diced
Chopped fresh coriander
3 Tbsps tarragon or sherry vinegar
Salt and pepper
Pinch of cayenne pepper
3 Tbsps olive oil
Whole coriander leaves, to garnish

Skin the salmon fillet and cut the fish into 1-inch pieces. Place in a bowl and add the vinegar, stirring well. Leave to stand for at least 2 hours.

Cut the vegetables into 1/2-inch dice and place the carrots in boiling water for about 5 minutes. Add the zucchini and turnip during the last minute of cooking time. Add the coriander, oil, salt, pepper and pinch of cayenne pepper to the fish. Combine with the vegetables, mixing carefully so the fish does not break up. Chill the mixture briefly before serving, and garnish with coriander.
Time: Preparation takes about 30 minutes, plus 2 hours for the salmon to marinate.
Cook's Tip: Fish allowed to marinate in vinegar, lemon or lime juice will appear opaque and "cooked" after about 2 hours.

Salade aux Fruits de Mer

This classic French salad is perfect for an open-air meal.

SERVES 4

Salad

8 scallops with roe attached

8 oz cooked shrimp, peeled

½ pint mussels

8 oz monkfish

Lemon juice

1 head Romaine lettuce

2 heads Belgian endive

Dressing

3 oz package cream cheese

⅔ cup plain yogurt

Juice of 1 lemon

3 Tbsps milk

1 Tbsp Dijon mustard

1 Tbsp chopped fresh tarragon

1 Tbsp chopped fresh chives

1 Tbsp chopped fresh parsley

Salt and pepper

Poach scallops and monkfish in lemon juice and enough water to cover, for about 5 minutes until just firm. Leave to cool in the liquid. Scrub the mussels well and put into a covered saucepan with 4 tablespoons of water. Shake pan over heat for about 5 minutes, or until the shells open. Discard any mussels whose shells remain closed. Remove the mussels from their shells and set aside. When scallops and monkfish are cool cut scallops in half, horizontally, and cut monkfish into 1-inch pieces. Mix all the fish and shellfish together. Remove the core from the Belgian endive, separate the leaves and wash and dry well. Wash the Romaine lettuce, remove the core and shred finely.

To make the dressing, blend cheese and milk in a blender or food processor. Add lemon juice, salt and pepper to taste, and mustard, and stir in the chopped herbs. Arrange the endive leaves on serving plates. Pile the shredded lettuce on top, leaving points of endive leaves showing. Toss the shellfish in half the dressing and pile on top of the lettuce. Put another spoonful of dressing on top of each serving and serve any remaining dressing separately.

Time: Preparation takes 20 minutes and cooking takes 10 minutes.

Shrimp in Melon

Deliciously cool and refreshing for a summer lunch, this recipe could also be served as an unusual appetizer for eight people.

SERVES 4

2 small melons

4 tomatoes

1 small cucumber

1 orange

Juice of half a lemon

4 Tbsps light vegetable oil

3 Tbsps heavy cream

2 Tbsps chopped fresh mint, reserve 4 sprigs for garnish

Pinch of sugar

Salt and pepper

1 tsp chopped fresh lemon thyme (optional)

1¼ cups shrimp, cooked and peeled

¾ cup toasted slivered almonds

Cut the melons in half through the middle, remove the seeds and scoop out the flesh with a melon baller or spoon. Leave a ¼-inch border of fruit on the inside of each shell. Cut the melon flesh into ½-inch cubes, or leave in balls. Peel the tomatoes and remove the seeds. Cut the flesh into strips. Peel the cucumber, cut into half lengthways and then into ½-inch cubes. Peel and segment the orange.

In a large bowl, mix together the lemon juice, oil, and heavy cream. Stir in the mint, sugar, salt, pepper, and thyme, if using. Add the shrimp and the fruit and vegetables, and mix thoroughly to coat evenly with the dressing. Pile equal quantities of the fruit and shrimp mixture into the two shells and chill well. Serve garnished with the reserved mint sprigs and the almonds.

Time: Preparation takes about 25 minutes. Allow at least 2 hours for chilling the salad, before serving.

Preparation: If the melon shells will not stand upright, cut a thin slice off the bottom of each one to make them more stable.

Serving Idea: Serve with a mixed green salad and new potatoes.

Crab & Citrus Salad

A lovely combination of flavors turns crab into something special.

SERVES 4

1 large crab or 8 oz crab meat
2 oranges
2 lemons
2 limes
1 pink grapefruit
1 small iceberg lettuce
²/₃ cup plain yogurt
¹/₃ cup heavy cream
1 Tbsp chili sauce
¹/₂ Tbsp brandy
Pinch of cayenne pepper
Salt
2 Tbsps salad oil

Separate the body from the shell of the crab, and remove and discard lungs and stomach sac. Chop the body into 3 or 4 pieces with a very sharp knife and pick out the meat. Scrape brown meat from inside shell and add to body meat. Break off large claws and remove meat from legs. Crack the claws and remove claw meat. Mix all the meat together and reserve legs for garnish. (If using canned or frozen crab meat, pick over the meat to remove any bits of shell or cartilage.)

Mix together yogurt, chili sauce, cream, brandy, cayenne pepper, and a pinch of salt, and toss with the crab meat. Take a thin strip of peel from each of the citrus fruits, scraping off the bitter white part. Cut each strip of peel into thin slivers. Put into boiling water and allow to boil for about 1 minute. Drain, refresh under cold water, and set aside. Peel each of the citrus fruits and cut into segments; do all this over a bowl to reserve juices. Add 2 tablespoons salad oil to the juice in the bowl, and toss with citrus segments. Shred the iceberg lettuce and arrange on plates. Put the crab meat in its dressing on top of lettuce. Arrange citrus segments over and around crab meat and sprinkle citrus peel over the top.
Time: Preparation takes 20 minutes.

Spanish Rice & Sole Salad

A complete meal in itself, this salad is ideal for a summer lunch.

SERVES 4

2 large lemon sole, each filleted into 4 pieces

4-6 peppercorns

Slice of onion

1 Tbsp lemon juice

¾ cup long grain rice

1 small eggplant

2 Tbsps olive oil

1 red bell pepper, chopped into ¼-inch dice

1 shallot, finely chopped

1 green bell pepper, chopped into ¼-inch dice

3 Tbsps French dressing

1 Tbsp chopped fresh mixed herbs

1 cup mayonnaise

1 clove garlic, finely chopped

1 tsp tomato paste

1 tsp paprika

Salt and pepper

2 bunches watercress, to garnish

Lay the sole fillets in an ovenproof dish, together with the peppercorns, slice of onion, lemon juice, and just enough water to cover. Sprinkle with a little salt and cover the dish with foil or a lid. Poach in a preheated 350°F oven for 8-10 minutes, or until fish is opaque. Allow the fish to cool in the liquor, then cut each fillet into ½-inch pieces.

Cook the rice in boiling water until soft. Rinse in cold water and separate the grains with a fork. Cut the eggplant in half and sprinkle with 2 teaspoons salt. Allow to stand for 30 minutes, then rinse very thoroughly. Pat dry and cut into ½-inch dice.

Heat the oil in a large skillet, and fry the eggplant until it is soft. Allow the eggplant to cool, then mix it into the rice along with the shallot, peppers, half the chopped herbs, and the French dressing. Mix together the mayonnaise, garlic, tomato paste, paprika, remaining herbs, and seasoning. Arrange the rice on one side of a serving dish and the sole pieces on the other. Spoon the mayonnaise over the sole and garnish the dish with watercress.

Time: Preparation takes about 20 minutes and cooking takes 15-20 minutes.

Freezing: Rice can be cooked and frozen in convenient amounts. To use, the frozen rice should be put straight into boiling water and allowed to cook for 3-4 minutes, then rinsed in cold water.

Shrimp Remoulade

Ensure you use only the very freshest shrimp for this recipe.

SERVES 4

3 Tbsps French mustard mixed with 2 tsps horseradish

1 Tbsp paprika

1 fresh chili, seeded and finely chopped

1 clove garlic, finely chopped

Salt

½ cup white wine vinegar

1½ cups oil

6 green onions, sliced

2 stalks celery, thinly sliced

2 bay leaves

2 Tbsps chopped fresh parsley

1½ pounds fresh, raw, unshelled large shrimp

Lettuce and lemon wedges, to serve

Combine the mustard, paprika, chili, garlic, and salt in a deep bowl. Mix in the vinegar thoroughly. Add the oil in a thin, steady stream while beating constantly with a small whisk. Continue to beat until the sauce is smooth and thick. Add the green onions, celery, bay leaves, and chopped parsley. Cover the bowl tightly and leave in the refrigerator for several hours, or overnight. Shell the shrimp, except for the very tail ends. If desired, the shrimp may be completely shelled. Two hours before serving, add the shrimp to the marinade and stir to coat them well. Refrigerate until ready to serve. To serve, shred the lettuce finely and place on individual serving plates. Arrange the shrimp on top and spoon over some of the marinade, discarding the bay leaves. Garnish with lemon wedges.

Time: Preparation takes about 25 minutes, plus at least 2 hours chilling.

Bean, Nut, & Shrimp Salad

This delicious combination of ingredients is perfect picnic fare.

SERVES 4

1 pound green beans, trimmed

¾ pound cooked jumbo shrimp

¼ cup whole hazelnuts, skinned

1 red bell pepper, thinly sliced

½ cup olive oil

3 Tbsps white wine vinegar

1 tsp Dijon mustard

1 Tbsp chopped fresh parsley

1 small head iceberg lettuce, shredded

Salt and pepper

Toast hazelnuts in a preheated 350°F oven for about 15 minutes, or until golden brown. Allow to cool, then chop coarsely. Bring salted water to a boil in a saucepan, and cook the beans in it for about 4-6 minutes – they should remain crisp. Drain, refresh under cold water, drain again and dry. Cook pepper slices in boiling water for about 1 minute. Drain and refresh under cold water, and allow to dry. Whisk the oil, vinegar, Dijon mustard, and seasonings together. Peel the shrimp, and mix together with beans, pepper, hazelnuts, and dressing. Arrange the lettuce on individual serving dishes, and pile shrimp mixture on top. Sprinkle parsley over the top to serve.
Time: Preparation takes 15 minutes and cooking takes 20 minutes.

Shrimp Salad

Pasta just adds that little bit extra to salads and makes them go a whole lot further.

SERVES 4

3 cups pasta shells

Juice of 1 lemon

1 tsp paprika

½ cup mayonnaise

½ pound shrimp, cooked and shelled

Salt and pepper

1 lettuce

1 cucumber, sliced

Cook the pasta in plenty of boiling, salted water for 10 minutes, or until tender. Drain, and rinse under cold water. Shake off excess water, put pasta into a bowl, and pour over lemon juice. Leave to cool. Mix paprika into mayonnaise. Add to shrimp, add seasoning and toss. Arrange a bed of lettuce leaves and sliced cucumber in a dish, and pile pasta in center. Pile the shrimp on top.
Time: Preparation takes 10 minutes and cooking takes 15 minutes.
Variation: This salad can also be made with flaked crab meat or salmon.
Serving Idea: Serve this salad on a bed of lettuce and herbs.

Lobster Salad

No book on seafood would be complete without a lobster salad.

SERVES 3-4

Salad

1 large cooked lobster

2 cooked chicken breasts

4 stalks celery

½ cup browned cashew nuts

4 green onions

1 head Chinese cabbage

1 head curly endive

4 oz snow peas

Garnish

1 red bell pepper, thinly sliced

2 Tbsps chopped fresh parsley

Dressing

1¼ cups mayonnaise

2 Tbsps soy sauce

1 tsp honey

Sesame oil

½ tsp ground ginger

1 Tbsp dry sherry (optional)

Twist off the claws and legs of the lobster. Cut the body in half, take out the tail meat and set aside. Crack claws and remove meat. Remove as much meat as possible from all the legs. Cut chicken breast meat into thin, even slices. Reserve the meat from 1 breast and mix the remaining shredded chicken with the meat from the lobster claws and legs. Cut lobster tail meat lengthwise into 3-4 thin slices. Set lobster tail meat aside with the reserved chicken meat. Mix celery, cashew nuts, and green onions together with the shredded lobster and chicken. Mix the dressing ingredients together, adding ground black pepper and salt if necessary. Mix the dressing with the shredded lobster and chicken. Slice the bell pepper into thin strips. Slice the Chinese cabbage into thin strips. Tear the curly endive leaves into pieces. Pile the greens and snow peas onto a large serving dish and mound the shredded lobster and chicken salad in the middle. Arrange some sliced chicken breast and the lobster tail neatly over the top. Garnish with sliced bell pepper and chopped parsley. Serve any remaining dressing separately.

Time: Preparation takes 25 minutes.

Red Snapper Niçoise

The attractive appearance of red snapper lends itself to this colorful dish.

SERVES 4

2 Tbsps red wine vinegar
½ cup olive oil
¼ tsp French mustard
Handful of chopped fresh mixed herbs
1 shallot, finely chopped
1 clove garlic, finely chopped
Salt and pepper
1 cup button mushrooms, quartered
4 red snapper, descaled and cleaned
Seasoned all-purpose flour
Lemon juice
1 pound tomatoes, quartered and cores removed
1 green bell pepper, sliced
¼ cup pitted black olives, halved
2 hard-cooked eggs, quartered
Small can anchovy fillets

In a screw top jar, shake together the vinegar, 6 tablespoons of the olive oil, the mustard, herbs, shallot, garlic, and seasoning, to make a French dressing. Put the mushrooms into a bowl and pour over the French dressing. Stir to coat the mushrooms evenly and refrigerate for about 1 hour.

Toss the snapper in the seasoned flour to coat lightly. Heat the remaining oil in a skillet and fry the fish on both sides for 2-3 minutes per side, until fish is firm but still moist. Sprinkle lightly with lemon juice and salt and pepper, and allow to go cold. When ready to serve, add the tomatoes, pepper, olives, and eggs to the mushrooms. Stir together gently, to coat the salad with the dressing. Pile the salad onto a serving dish and arrange the red snapper on top. Garnish with the drained anchovy fillets.

Time: Preparation takes 15 minutes and cooking takes 15 minutes.

Cook's Tip: The French dressing is delicious with other salads, so make extra. It will keep in a screw top jar in the refrigerator for up to 2 weeks.

Crab Meat Imperial

This makes a delicious warm weather salad for lunches, light suppers or elegant appetizers.

SERVES 2-4

2 small crabs, boiled, or 1½ cups crab meat
2 Tbsps oil
4 green onions
1 small green bell pepper, finely chopped
1 stalk celery, finely chopped
1 clove garlic, finely chopped
¾ cup prepared mayonnaise
1 Tbsp mild mustard
Dash Tabasco and Worcestershire sauce
1 piece canned pimiento, drained and finely chopped
Salt and pepper
2 Tbsps chopped fresh parsley
Lettuce, curly endive or raddichio (optional)

To shell the crabs, first remove all the legs and the large claws by twisting and pulling them away from the body. Turn the shell over and, using your thumbs, push the body away from the flat shell. Set the body aside. Remove the stomach sack and the lungs or dead man's fingers and discard them. Using a small teaspoon, scrape the brown body meat out of the flat shell. Using a sharp knife, cut the body of the crab in four pieces and using a pick or a skewer, push out all the meat. Crack the large claws and remove the meat in one piece if possible. Crack the legs and remove the meat, leaving the small, thin legs in the shell. Set all the meat aside. Scrub the shells if using for serving.

Heat the oil in a small skillet. Chop the white parts of the green onions and add to the oil with the green bell pepper, celery, and garlic. Sauté over gentle heat for about 10 minutes, stirring often to soften the vegetables but not brown them. Remove from the heat and set aside. When cool, add the mayonnaise, mustard, Tabasco, Worcestershire sauce, pimiento, some salt and pepper, and finely chopped tops of the green onions. Spoon the reserved brown body meat from the crabs back into each shell or serving dish. Gently mix the remaining crab meat with the dressing, reserving the claws for garnish, if desired, or shredding and adding to the other crab meat. Spoon into the shells on top of the brown body meat, and sprinkle with chopped parsley. Place the crab shells on serving plates, surround them with lettuce leaves and garnish with the shelled crab claws and crab legs if desired.

Time: Preparation takes about 45 minutes and cooking takes 10 minutes.

Trout with Pine Nut Stuffing

Bacon and pine nut stuffing adds a lovely flavor to the fish in this simple recipe.

SERVES 4

4 whole trout, cleaned

Stuffing

2 strips bacon

½ cup pine nuts

2 Tbsps chopped chives

1 cup white bread crumbs

2 Tbsps cream

Salt and pepper

Chop the bacon into small pieces. Heat a skillet over a medium heat and fry the bacon until crisp. Add the pine nuts and cook gently for 1 minute. Add the remaining ingredients, mix together well and remove from the heat.

Stuff each fish with the bacon and pine nut mixture, pushing the stuffing well into the cavity. Do not over-stuff the fish as this will cause it to burst open during cooking. Barbecue the fish for about 6 minutes on each side until tender, basting with butter or oil occasionally to keep it moist.

Time: Preparation takes 5 minutes and cooking takes 12-15 minutes.

Grilled Garlic Shrimp

This simple treatment is especially delicious.

SERVES 4

2 pounds uncooked jumbo shrimp

4 Tbsps melted butter

Marinade

3 cloves garlic, finely chopped

4 Tbsps oil

½ cup lemon juice

4 Tbsps chopped fresh basil

Salt

Coarsely ground black pepper

Shell and de-vein the shrimp. Leave the shells on the ends of the tails. Combine the marinade ingredients in a plastic bag. Add the shrimp and seal the bag. Refrigerate for 1 hour, turning frequently. Place the bag in a bowl to catch possible drips. Drain the shrimp and thread onto 4 skewers. Mix the marinade with the melted butter and brush the shrimp with the mixture. Grill for 8-10 minutes, about 4-6 inches above the coals, until the shrimp are pink and firm. Brush frequently with the marinade while the shrimp cook. Pour over remaining marinade before serving.

Time: Preparation takes 15 minutes and cooking takes 8-10 minutes.

Sardines with Lemon & Oregano

Sardines are supreme barbecue food as they cook so well over coals.

SERVES 4-6

8-12 fresh sardines, cleaned, scaled, washed and dried

8-12 sprigs fresh oregano

⅓ cup olive oil

Juice and rind of 2 lemons

Salt and pepper

1 Tbsp dried oregano

Place a sprig of oregano inside each fish. Mix the oil, lemon juice, rind, and salt and pepper together. Make two slits on each side of the fish. Brush the fish with the lemon mixture and grill over hot coals for 3-4 minutes per side, basting frequently, until lightly browned. When the fish are nearly done, sprinkle the dried oregano on the coals. The smoke will give the fish extra flavor.

Time: Preparation takes 15 minutes and cooking takes 6-8 minutes.

Scallop & Shrimp — Kebabs —

Serve these delightful kebabs with a simple green salad.

SERVES 6

24 scallops

24 uncooked jumbo shrimp, peeled and de-veined

4 limes, cut into wedges

Pepper

Lime butter sauce

2 egg yolks

1 Tbsp lime juice

Grated rind of 1 lime

⅔ cup butter

1 Tbsp finely chopped fresh dill

Thread the scallops, shrimp, and lime wedges onto skewers. Season and set aside while preparing the sauce.

In the top of a double boiler combine the egg yolks, lime juice and rind. Place over boiling water and gradually whisk in small pieces of butter until the sauce thickens. Remove from the heat and add the dill. Spread a little of the sauce on the kebabs and heat them over the coals until tender, basting often with the sauce.

Time: Preparation takes about 25 minutes and cooking takes 8-10 minutes for the kebabs.

Gray Mullet with Fennel

Fennel adds a lovely flavor to fish.

SERVES 4

2-4 gray mullet, depending upon size, cleaned

Marinade

⅓ cup oil

1 Tbsp fennel seeds, slightly crushed

1 clove garlic, finely chopped

Juice and rind of 1 lemon

2 Tbsps chopped fennel tops

Salt and pepper

Heat the oil, add the fennel seeds and cook for one minute. Add the garlic and remaining ingredients except the fennel tops. Leave the mixture to cool completely. Place the fish in a shallow dish and pour over the marinade. Cover and refrigerate for 1 hour. Grill the fish over hot coals 10-12 minutes per side until lightly browned. Sprinkle over fennel tops halfway through cooking.

Time: Preparation takes 15 minutes and cooking takes about 20 minutes.

Cook's Tip: Fennel tops may also be placed directly on the coals for aromatic smoke.

Swordfish Steaks with Peppercorns

The sauce in this recipe goes well with many types of fish.

SERVES 4

2 Tbsps fresh green peppercorns

6 Tbsps lemon juice

4 Tbsps olive oil

Salt

4 swordfish steaks

Sauce

1 egg

1 clove garlic, chopped

½ cup oil

1 Tbsp lemon juice

2 sprigs fresh oregano

Salt and pepper

Crush the green peppercorns slightly and mix with lemon juice, oil, and salt. Place the swordfish steaks in a shallow dish and pour over the lemon and oil mixture. Cover and refrigerate several hours, turning frequently. Process the egg and garlic in a blender or food processor. With the machine running, pour oil through the funnel in a thin, steady stream. When the sauce is thick, strip the leaves off the oregano and process to chop them finely. Add lemon juice, salt, and pepper. Grill the swordfish over hot coals for 15 minutes, basting frequently and turning once. Serve with the sauce. (Peppercorns will pop when exposed to the heat of the grill.)

Time: Preparation takes 25 minutes and cooking takes 15 minutes.

Monkfish & Pepper Kebabs

A wonderfully rich sauce transforms kebabs into something very special.

SERVES 4

2 pounds monkfish, cut into 2-inch pieces

8 strips bacon

2 pieces lemon grass

1 green bell pepper, cut into 2-inch pieces

1 red bell pepper, cut into 2-inch pieces

12 button mushrooms

8 bay leaves

Oil

Bearnaise butter sauce

½ cup dry white wine

4 Tbsps tarragon vinegar

2 shallots, finely chopped

1 Tbsp chopped fresh tarragon

1 Tbsp chopped fresh chervil or parsley

1 cup butter, softened

Salt and pepper

Cut the bacon in half lengthwise and again in half across. Peel the lemon grass and use only the core. Cut into small pieces. Place a piece of fish on each strip of bacon and top with a piece of lemon grass. Roll up. Thread the rolls of fish onto skewers, alternating with the bell peppers, mushrooms, and bay leaves. Brush with oil and broil for 15 minutes, or until fish looks opaque, turning and basting often. While the fish cooks, heat the white wine, vinegar, and shallots in a small saucepan until boiling. Cook rapidly to reduce by half. Add the herbs and lower the heat. Beat in the softened butter a bit at a time until the sauce is the thickness of hollandaise sauce. Season with salt and pepper to taste and serve with the fish kebabs.

Time: Preparation takes 30 minutes and cooking takes 25 minutes.

Fish Kebabs with -Horseradish-

The strong flavor of horseradish is perfectly suited to smoked fish.

SERVES 4

1 smoked kipper fillet, skinned and cut into 1-inch pieces
1 smoked haddock fillet, skinned and cut into 1-inch pieces
8 bay leaves
1 small Spanish onion, quartered
Oil
Sauce
2 Tbsps grated fresh or bottled horseradish
1 cup sour cream
2 tsps fresh dill, chopped
Salt and pepper
Squeeze of lemon juice
Pinch of sugar

Thread the fish, bay leaves, and slices of onion onto skewers, alternating ingredients and types of fish. Brush with oil and place on an oiled grill rack above hot coals. Mix the sauce ingredients together and divide onto side plates. Grill the kebabs for about 6 minutes until fish looks opaque, turning and basting with oil frequently. When the onion is cooked, remove the kebabs to serving dishes. Place kebabs on lettuce leaves, if desired, for serving.
Time: Preparation takes 15 minutes and cooking takes 6 minutes.

Marsala Fish

Inspired by the flavors of India, this recipe will add an unusual twist to your barbecue.

SERVES 4

4 medium-sized mackerel, trout or similar fish
Juice of 1 lemon
2 tsps turmeric
2 green chilies, finely chopped
1 small piece fresh ginger root, peeled and grated
1 clove garlic, finely chopped
Pinch of ground cinnamon
Pinch of ground cloves
4 Tbsps oil
Salt and pepper
Fresh coriander leaves
Accompaniment
½ cucumber, finely diced
½ cup thick plain yogurt
1 green onion, finely chopped
Salt and pepper

Clean the fish and cut three slits on each side of the fish. Combine the spices, lemon juice, oil, garlic, and chili peppers and spread over the fish and inside the cuts. Place whole sprigs of coriander inside the fish. Brush the grill rack lightly with oil or use a wire fish rack. Cook the fish 10-15 minutes until browned, turning often and basting with any remaining mixture. Combine the accompaniment ingredients and serve with the fish.
Time: Preparation takes 25 minutes and cooking takes 10-15 minutes.

Zanzibar Shrimp

Shrimp and pineapple are particularly good enhanced with a sweet sauce.

SERVES 4

1 pound uncooked jumbo shrimp

1 large fresh pineapple, peeled, cored, and cut into chunks

Oil

Sauce

½ cup orange juice

1 Tbsp vinegar

1 Tbsp lime juice

1 tsp dry mustard

1 Tbsp brown sugar

Remaining pineapple

Garnish

Flaked coconut

Curly endive

Shell and de-vein the shrimp. Thread the shrimp and pineapple pieces on skewers, alternating each ingredient. Use about 4 pineapple pieces per skewer. Place the remaining pineapple and the sauce ingredients into a food processor and purée. Pour into a small pan and cook over low heat for about 10-15 minutes to reduce slightly. Place the kebabs on a lightly oiled rack above the coals and cook about 6 minutes, basting frequently with the sauce. Sprinkle the cooked kebabs with coconut and serve on endive leaves. Serve remaining sauce separately.

Time: Preparation takes 25 minutes and cooking takes about 20 minutes.

Red Snapper with Tarragon

Whole fish is a must for the barbecue.

SERVES 4

4 large or 8 small red snapper, scaled, washed, and dried

4 or 8 sprigs fresh tarragon

Marinade

4 Tbsps oil

2 Tbsps tarragon vinegar

Salt and pepper

Sauce

1 egg

½ cup oil

1 tsp Dijon mustard

1 Tbsp each chopped fresh tarragon and parsley

1 Tbsp tarragon vinegar

2 Tbsps heavy cream

1 tsp brandy

Place a sprig of tarragon inside each fish. Cut two slits on the side of each fish. Mix the marinade ingredients together, pour over the fish and refrigerate for 30 minutes, covered. Put the egg in a food processor. Add the mustard, salt and pepper and process to mix. Add the oil through the funnel, with the machine running, in a thin, steady stream. Add the herbs, vinegar, and brandy and process to mix well. Fold in the heavy cream and pour into a serving dish. Set aside. Grill the fish for 5-8 minutes per side until lightly browned, basting frequently with the marinade while cooking. Serve with the sauce.

Time: Preparation takes 15 minutes and cooking takes 10-15 minutes.

Entrées

Seafood entrées come in various guises. At one time a whole baked fish was considered the classic centerpiece with which to impress guests. Today, however, we are all becoming much more adventurous and, as a result, a far greater diversity of seafood recipes are gracing our tables. The ornate treatment given to salmon to produce Salmon Amandine is still very worthwhile for special occasions – the fish is covered with almond "scales," each laid on individually – but in these days when we all seem to want fresh food fast, such simple dishes as Grilled Tuna and Rosemary are coming to the fore.

When choosing an entrée think first of the balance of flavors in a meal. This is crucially important if one course is not to clash with another. Most people choose their entrée first and then build the other courses around this, but this is by no means a rule. If you want to feature a particular appetizer, for instance, there is nothing to prevent you choosing your entrée to complement it. This is not too much of a problem, unless you choose something with a particularly strong flavor. The main consideration for many people is to avoid too many rich ingredients or serving too much of the same thing. If you were serving a simple entrée such as Boston Scrod, for example, it would be effective to balance this with a more complex appetizer.

This chapter features a wide variety of recipes specially chosen to cover a range of occasions. Obviously, depending on the guests, the season, and the setting, serving seafood as an entrée demands a variety of approaches. For an informal summer meal, for example, a refreshing dish such as Snapper with Fennel and Orange would be perfect, whereas the demands of a hoard of teenagers would probably be best satisfied with a spicy, easily accessible dish such as Crispy Fish with Chili. Serving seafood as an entrée does not limit you to serving whole fish or seafood. Combing it with pasta, for instance, to create a delicate Fish Ravioli will delight guests and make an expensive item go further. Similarly, the addition of salmon to a flan turns a very ordinary dish into something very special indeed.

As with all seafood recipes – perhaps even more so with entrées because so many of them are baked – it is vital not to rob the seafood of its moisture. Seafood must be moist to be enjoyable. When fish is cooked in oil or in any liquid this is usually not too much of a problem as the flesh is not subjected to fierce dry heat. With baked dishes, however, it is crucial to provide protection either by wrapping in foil or parchment or covering with a coating or marinade. All the recipes give precise instructions that avoid this but when it comes to adapting and creating your own dishes – which we hope you will do – always bear this in mind.

Grilled Tuna with — Rosemary —

A quick and easy way of serving sumptuous fresh tuna steaks.

SERVES 4

2 large tuna steaks
1 tsp chopped fresh rosemary
2 Tbsps bread crumbs
1 Tbsp chopped fresh parsley
1 clove garlic, finely chopped
2 Tbsps olive oil
2 lemons
Salt and pepper

Remove the bone from each tuna steak. Brush the steaks on one side with oil and sprinkle over half of the parsley, rosemary, garlic, bread crumbs, salt, and pepper. Preheat a heavy-based skillet and when hot, wipe over a little oil with a paper towel. Add the tuna steaks, herbed side down. Quickly brush the tops of the steaks with the remaining oil, and sprinkle over the remaining parsley, rosemary, garlic, bread crumbs, and a little salt and pepper. Turn the steaks to cook other side. Cook the tuna to your liking. Serve immediately, accompanied by lemon halves.
Time: Preparation takes about 10 minutes and cooking takes 8-12 minutes.
Serving Idea: Serve with a tossed green salad and mayonnaise.

Swordfish Florentine

This recipe has a distinctly Mediterranean flavor.

SERVES 4

4 swordfish steaks about 6-8 oz each in weight
Salt, pepper, and lemon juice
Olive oil
2 pounds fresh spinach, stems removed and leaves well washed

Aioli sauce

2 egg yolks
1-2 cloves garlic
Salt, pepper, and dry mustard
Pinch of cayenne pepper
1 cup olive oil
Lemon juice or white wine vinegar

Sprinkle fish with pepper, lemon juice, and olive oil. Place under a broiler and cook for about 3-4 minutes per side.

Meanwhile, shred the spinach finely. Place in a large saucepan and add a pinch of salt. Cover and cook over moderate heat for about 2 minutes with only the water that clings to the leaves after washing. Set aside. Place egg yolks in a food processor with the garlic. Process several times to mix eggs and purée garlic. Add salt, pepper, mustard, and cayenne pepper. With the machine running, pour oil through the funnel in a thin, steady stream. When the sauce becomes very thick, add some lemon juice or vinegar in small quantities. Place a bed of spinach on a plate and top with the swordfish. Spoon some of the aioli sauce on top of the fish and serve the rest separately.
Time: Preparation takes 25 minutes and cooking takes 6-8 minutes.

Salmon Amandine

It takes a little time to produce the almond "scales" on the salmon, but the end result is well worth the effort.

SERVES 8

5-6 pound whole salmon, cleaned

Court bouillon

4 cups water

3 stalks celery, diced

1 onion, quartered and stuck with whole cloves

Stuffing

6 cups crushed Ritz crackers

5 Tbsps butter, melted

¾ cup cream sherry

2 tsps salt

2 tsps Worcestershire sauce

2 drops Tabasco sauce

1½ pounds Maine crab meat

Garnish

1 pound blanched, sliced almonds

1 egg white

Cut the underside of the salmon from the end of the slit from where it was cleaned, up to the tip of the tail. Set the fish belly-side down and spread out the cut underside. Press down along the backbone of the fish, pushing the spine downwards. Turn the fish over and pull the backbone away using a sharp knife, then cut it out at the base of the head and tail using a pair of scissors. Combine the fish bones with the court bouillon ingredients in a saucepan. Bring to a boil and simmer for 20 minutes, then allow to cool while preparing the stuffing.

Combine all the stuffing ingredients and mix well. Spoon the stuffing into the cavity of the salmon. Brush the fish with melted butter and place in the top of the fish steamer or in a roasting pan. If using a roasting pan, carefully pour the cooled court bouillon over the fish. Cover with foil and steam in a preheated 350°F oven for about 50 minutes. When the fish is done the flesh will look opaque and flake easily. Remove the fish from the steamer or roasting pan and peel the skin from one side of the fish from the head to the tail, leaving the head and tail intact. Garnish the side of the fish with the almonds, using egg white to hold them in place, to give the fish a scale effect. Brown under a preheated broiler until golden.

Time: Preparation takes 45 minutes and cooking takes 50 minutes.

Fish Ravioli

Ravioli stuffed with fish is a little unusual, but it tastes absolutely wonderful.

SERVES 4

Filling

½ pound sole fillets, or other flat fish, skinned and boned

1 slice of onion

1 slice of lemon

6 peppercorns

1 bay leaf

1 Tbsp lemon juice

1¼ cups water

2 eggs, beaten

2 Tbsps bread crumbs

1 green onion, finely chopped

Dough

2 cups all-purpose flour

Pinch of salt

3 eggs

Lemon sauce

2 Tbsps butter

2 Tbsps all-purpose flour

1¼ cups strained cooking liquid from fish

2 Tbsps heavy cream

Salt and pepper

2 Tbsps lemon juice

Wash and dry the fish. Place in ovenproof dish with slice of onion, slice of lemon, peppercorns, bay leaf, lemon juice, and water. Cover and cook in a preheated 350°F oven for 20 minutes, or until the flesh is opaque and flakes easily. Remove fish from liquid and allow to drain. Strain liquid, and set aside. When fish is cool, beat with the back of a spoon to a pulp. Add eggs, bread crumbs, and green onions, and salt and pepper to taste. Mix well and set aside.

Sift flour into a bowl and add the salt. Make a well in the center, and add the eggs. Work the flour and eggs together with a spoon, and then knead by hand, until a smooth dough is formed. Leave to rest for 15 minutes. Lightly flour a board, and roll out dough thinly into a rectangle. Cut dough in half. Shape the filling into small balls, and set them about 1½ inches apart on one half of the dough. Place the other half on top, and cut with a ravioli cutter or small pastry cutter. Seal the edges.

Cook in batches in a large, wide pan with plenty of boiling, salted water until tender – about 8 minutes. Remove carefully with a perforated spoon. Meanwhile, make the sauce. Melt butter in pan, stir in flour, and cook for 30 seconds. Draw off the heat and gradually stir in liquid from cooked fish. Return to heat and bring to a boil. Simmer for 4 minutes, stirring continuously. Add cream and mix well. Season to taste. Remove from heat, and gradually stir in lemon juice. Do not reboil. Pour sauce over ravioli and serve immediately.

Time: Preparation takes 30 minutes and cooking takes 30 minutes.

Watchpoint: Stir the white sauce thoroughly when adding the milk or it will form lumps.

Sole with Belgian Endive

Sole and sautéed endive make a tasty flavor combination.

SERVES 6

3 sole

12 thin slices bacon, finely sliced

6 heads of Belgian endive

1½ cups heavy cream

3 Tbsps butter

Fresh dill

Salt and pepper

Pull the skins (white and black) off the sole. Cut along the backbone and remove the fillets. Wrap the fillets in plastic wrap and press flat with the blade of a large chopping knife. Cut the bacon slices to fit the fillets exactly. Save the trimmings. Season with pepper. Roll up neatly and tightly. Place each roll on a piece of plastic wrap. Fold it up and over the rolled fillets, twisting the two ends to close. Separate all the endive leaves, wash, dry, and cut in fine julienne.

Bring the cream to a boil. Blend smooth with a hand-held electric blender, then add the bacon. Keep warm over hot water. Cook the rolled fillets in a steamer for 10 minutes. Heat the butter in a pan. When foaming, sauté the endive over a high heat. Season the endive with salt and pepper. When cooked (approximately 3 minutes), set aside. When the rolled fillets are cooked, remove the plastic wrap and slice into round slices. Place the slices on a bed of endive with the reheated sauce. Sprinkle with chopped dill and serve.

Time: Preparation takes 1 hour and cooking takes 20 minutes.

Salmon with Cucumber Cream

This subtle sauce complements the salmon perfectly.

SERVES 4

4 salmon cutlets (tail pieces)

2 Tbsps butter

1 small cucumber

2 Tbsps light broth

⅔ cup milk

2 Tbsps all-purpose flour

Salt and pepper

Lemon juice

Pinch of sugar

Nutmeg

¼ cup heavy cream

Grate the cucumber. Melt the butter in a saucepan, add half the cucumber, and cook slowly for about 10 minutes. Add the flour and stir to blend. Stir in the broth and milk, bring to a boil, then allow to cook slowly until the cucumber has softened. Put the contents of the pan into a blender or food processor and purée with the lemon juice, sugar, nutmeg, salt, and pepper until smooth. Stir in the remaining cucumber. Pour the cream over the top of the hot sauce and set aside in a saucepan while cooking the fish. Skin the cutlets and put into a baking dish with water and seasoning. Poach in a preheated 350°F oven for 10 minutes, then remove from oven and keep warm. Re-heat the cucumber sauce, stir in the cream and allow to boil for 1 minute. Spoon some of the sauce onto serving plates and place the salmon cutlets on top. Coat with more of the sauce and serve.

Time: Preparation takes 15 minutes and cooking takes 20 minutes.

Eel in Red Wine

Eel can be bought ready-cleaned from the fish market if you don't want to do it yourself.

SERVES 4

1¼ pounds eel, skinned

Salt and pepper

2 Tbsps olive oil

2 onions, finely sliced

1 clove garlic, chopped

1¼ cups red wine

1 tsp sugar

3 Tbsps tomato paste

½ cup fish broth

Cut the eel into medium-thick slices and season with salt and pepper. Heat the oil and fry the onion and garlic for 1 minute. Add the eel slices to the pan and sear on both sides. Stir the wine and sugar into the pan, cook until the wine reduces, then add the tomato paste and the fish broth. Season with salt and pepper, if necessary. Transfer to an ovenproof dish and finish cooking in a preheated 375°F oven for 15 minutes, or until flesh is firm. Remove the eel from the dish and if the sauce is not very thick, pour it into a saucepan and thicken and reduce it over high heat. Serve the eel hot, with the sauce poured over.

Time: Preparation takes 20 minutes and cooking takes 25 minutes.

Sardine & Tomato Gratinée

Fresh sardines are becoming more widely available and this recipe makes the most of these delicious fish.

SERVES 4

3 Tbsps olive oil

2 pounds large fresh sardines, descaled and cleaned

2 leeks, cleaned and sliced

½ cup dry white wine

8 oz tomatoes, peeled and quartered

Salt and pepper

2 Tbsps each chopped fresh basil and parsley

½ cup Parmesan cheese, grated

½ cup dry bread crumbs

Heat the oil in a skillet and fry the sardines until they are brown on both sides. It may be necessary to do this in several batches, to prevent the fish from breaking up. When all the sardines are cooked, set them aside and cook the leeks gently in the sardine oil. When the leeks are soft, pour in the wine and boil rapidly until it is reduced by about two thirds. Add the tomatoes, seasoning, and herbs to the leeks and cook for about 1 minute. Pour the vegetables into an ovenproof dish and lay the sardines on top. Sprinkle the cheese and bread crumbs evenly over the sardines and bake in a preheated 425°F oven for about 5 minutes.

Time: Preparation takes 20-25 minutes and cooking takes about 15 minutes.

Red Snapper with Mushroom Sauce

Red snapper is often cooked with the liver left in – a delicacy.

SERVES 4

1 pound button mushrooms, left whole
1 clove garlic, finely chopped
3 Tbsps olive oil
Juice of 1 lemon
1 Tbsp finely chopped fresh parsley
2 tsps finely chopped fresh basil
1 tsp finely chopped fresh marjoram or sage
4 Tbsps dry white wine mixed with ½ tsp cornstarch
Few drops of anchovy paste
4 red snapper, each weighing about 8 oz
2 tsps white bread crumbs
2 tsps freshly grated Parmesan cheese

Combine the mushrooms, garlic, and olive oil in a small skillet. Cook over moderate heat for about 1 minute, until the garlic and mushrooms are slightly softened. Add all the herbs, the lemon juice, and white wine and cornstarch mixture. Bring to a boil and cook until thickened. Add anchovy paste to taste. Set aside while preparing the fish.

To clean the fish, cut along the stomach from the gills to the vent, the small hole near the tail. Clean out the cavity of the fish, leaving the liver, if desired. To remove the gills, lift the flap and snip them out with a sharp pair of scissors. Rinse the fish well and pat dry. Place the fish head to tail in a shallow ovenproof dish that can be used for serving. The fish should fit snugly into the dish.

Pour the prepared sauce over the fish and sprinkle with the bread crumbs and Parmesan cheese. Cover the dish loosely with foil and cook in the preheated 375°F oven, for about 20 minutes. The flesh will look opaque and flake easily when cooked. Uncover for the last 5 minutes, if desired, and raise the oven temperature slightly. This will lightly brown the fish.

Time: Preparation takes about 30 minutes, cooking takes about 25 minutes.

Preparation: If the fish need to be scaled, use the blunt edge of a knife and scrape from the tail to the head. Rinse well and remove any loose scales.

Fish Milanese

These fish, cooked in the style of Milan, have a crispy crumb coating and the fresh tang of lemon juice.

SERVES 4

8 sole or plaice fillets
2 Tbsps dry vermouth
1 bay leaf
6 Tbsps olive oil
Salt and pepper
Seasoned flour for coating
2 eggs, lightly beaten
Dry bread crumbs
Oil for shallow frying
6 Tbsps butter
1 clove garlic, finely chopped
2 tsps chopped fresh parsley
2 Tbsps capers
1 tsp chopped fresh oregano
Juice of 1 lemon
Salt and pepper
Lemon wedges and parsley, to garnish

Skin the fillets with a sharp filleting knife. Remove any small bones and place the fillets in a large, shallow dish. Combine the vermouth, oil, and bay leaf in a small saucepan and heat gently. Allow to cool completely and pour over the fish. Leave the fish to marinate for about 1 hour, turning them occasionally. Remove the fish from the marinade and coat lightly with the seasoned flour. Dip the fillets into the beaten eggs to coat or, alternatively, use a pastry brush to brush the eggs onto the fillets. Dip the egg-coated fillet into the bread crumbs, pressing the crumbs on firmly.

Heat the oil in a large skillet. Add the fillets and cook slowly on both sides until golden brown – about 3 minutes on each side. Remove and drain on paper towels. Pour the oil out of the skillet and wipe it clean. Add the butter and the garlic and cook until both turn a light brown. Add the herbs, capers, and lemon juice and pour immediately over the fish. Garnish with lemon wedges and sprigs of parsley.

Time: Preparation takes 1 hour for the fish to marinate, cooking takes about 6 minutes.

Cook's Tip: If necessary, keep the fish fillets warm by placing on a wire cooling rack covered with paper towels and place in a warm oven, leaving the door slightly ajar. Sprinkling the fish fillets lightly with salt as they drain on paper towels helps remove some of the oil.

Baked Sea Trout in Parchment

Baking fish *en papillote*, or in paper parcels, preserves all the wonderful flavor and juices. The parcels are opened at the table for full effect.

SERVES 2

1-1¼ pounds sea trout fillet

2 sheets baking paper or foil

4 slices Spanish onion

4 slices fresh tomato

4 rings green bell pepper

4 mussels, cleaned and debearded

4 sprigs of fresh thyme and sage

2 white peppercorns, crushed

Melted butter

White wine

Divide the fish into two equal portions and place, skinned side down, on two sheets of baking paper. Garnish the fish with onion slices, tomato slices, and pepper rings. Place the mussels on top and then the herbs and pepper. Drizzle a little melted butter and wine on the fish and then seal the paper parcels, twisting the ends well. Coat the outside with additional melted butter and bake in a preheated 350°F oven for about 20 minutes. Time: Preparation takes 25 minutes and cooking takes 20 minutes.

Perch & Shrimp Duet

This elegant fish dish is perfect for entertaining.

SERVES 6

18 raw jumbo shrimp, peeled and deveined

2 pounds ocean perch fillets, cut into bite-sized pieces

½ green bell pepper, thinly sliced

½ red bell pepper, thinly sliced

1 onion, finely chopped

1 tomato, peeled, seeded and chopped

1 zucchini, cut into thin rounds

5 Tbsps olive oil

1 clove garlic

Bouquet garni (parsley, thyme, bay leaf)

1⅛ cups fish broth

Fresh chervil

Salt and pepper

Cut the shrimp in two, lengthwise. In 3 tablespoons of olive oil, fry the onion and peppers for 3 minutes. Add the garlic, zucchini, and the tomato pulp. Mix well, fry for 5 minutes, and add the bouquet garni, salt, pepper, and fish broth. Cover and cook gently for 20 minutes, stirring frequently.

Heat 2 tablespoons of olive oil and sear the shrimp evenly all over for 3 minutes. Season. Drain on paper towels and keep warm in the oven. Place the fish fillets in a steamer. Season and cook, covered, for 5 minutes. Remove the bouquet garni from the vegetable mixture and blend to a smooth purée. Serve the fish fillets and shrimp with the vegetable purée sauce, garnished with the fresh chervil.

Time: Preparation takes 30 minutes and cooking takes 35 minutes.

Baked Stuffed — Mackerel —

This simple but tasty recipe will convert all those who consider mackerel a little too strongly flavored.

SERVES 4

¼ cup margarine
1 small onion, finely chopped
⅓ cup fresh whole-wheat bread crumbs
1½ tsps chopped fresh parsley
1 tsp dried thyme
Salt and pepper
2-3 Tbsps hot water if required
4 mackerel, cleaned and washed thoroughly

In a large skillet, melt the margarine. Fry the chopped onion in the margarine until it is soft, but not colored. Add the bread crumbs, herbs, and seasoning to the fried onion, and mix well to form a firm stuffing, adding a little hot water to bind, if necessary. Fill the cavities of the fish with the stuffing and wrap each one separately in well-oiled aluminum foil. Place each fish parcel on a cookie sheet, and cook in a preheated 375°F oven for 30 minutes, or until fish flakes easily.
Time: Preparation takes 15 minutes and cooking takes 30 minutes.

Crispy Fried — Catfish —

Eating catfish is a serious business in the South, and one taste of this Southern specialty will illustrate just why so many backwoods catfish restaurants still thrive.

SERVES 6

6 catfish
1 egg
½ cup evaporated milk
1 Tbsp salt
Pinch of pepper
1 cup all-purpose flour
½ cup yellow cornmeal
2 tsps paprika
Oil for frying

Clean, skin, wash, and dry the catfish before cutting them into serving-sized portions. Beat the egg into the milk and stir in the salt and pepper. In a separate bowl, combine the flour, cornmeal, and paprika. Dip the cleaned fish in the milk mixture, then roll in the seasoned flour. Heat the oil in a heavy-bottomed pan to 375°F or until a 1-inch cube of bread turns golden after 1 minute. When the oil is hot enough, add the fish and brown well on both sides. When the fish are done, lift them carefully from the pan and drain them on absorbent paper. Serve very hot.
Time: Preparation takes 45 minutes and cooking takes 10-15 minutes.

Salt Cod with Peppers

Salt cod is combined with peppers, chili, and garlic in this tasty recipe.

SERVES 6

2 pounds salt cod

2 red bell peppers

2 green bell peppers

3 large onions

6 cloves garlic

1 small red chili

5 large potatoes

3 Tbsps olive oil

4 Tbsps heavy cream

2 Tbsps chopped fresh parsley

2 tomatoes, peeled, seeded, and chopped

Salt and pepper

Fresh chervil, to garnish

Cut the salt cod into pieces. Soak in water for 24 hours, changing the water several times. Cut the peppers, remove the seeds and white part and slice into strips. Chop the onions finely. Chop the garlic. Seed and chop the chili pepper. Peel the potatoes, quarter them, and cook in boiling salted water for 30 minutes with 1 chopped onion and 1 tablespoon of olive oil.

Drain the potatoes and onions when cooled. Blend until smooth or press through a sieve. Add the cream and parsley, and season to taste. Bring the soaked and drained cod to a boil in a large quantity of water and cook for 5 minutes, or until opaque. Set aside to drain and cool. Flake with your fingers, discarding the skin and bones. Fry the chopped garlic and chili pepper in 3½ tablespoons oil until soft and lightly colored. Add the peppers and the two remaining onions. Cook for 10 minutes over a moderate heat, stirring well. Add the tomatoes to the peppers and onions, and cook for another 15 minutes, stirring frequently. Season to taste.

Oil the bottom of an ovenproof pan or individual pie dishes. Arrange a layer of the potato purée over the bottom. Spread the cod over it. Top with a layer of the pepper, onion, and tomato mixture. Bake in a preheated 400°F oven for 30 minutes. Serve hot, garnished with chopped chervil.

Time: Preparation takes 50 minutes, plus 24 hours soaking. Cooking takes 1 hour 20 minutes.

Paella

This dish has as many variations as Spain has cooks!

SERVES 6

12 mussels in their shells

6 clams

6 oz cod, skinned and cut into 2-inch pieces

12 large shrimp

3 chorizos or other spicy sausage

2 pound chicken, cut in 12 serving-size pieces

1 small onion, chopped

1 clove garlic, finely chopped

2 small bell peppers, red and green, shredded

1 pound long grain rice

Large pinch of saffron

Salt and pepper

4 cups boiling water

5 oz frozen peas

3 tomatoes, peeled, seeded, and chopped

Scrub the clams and mussels well to remove beards and barnacles. Discard any with broken shells or those that do not close when tapped. Leave the mussels and clams to soak in water with a handful of flour for 30 minutes. Remove the heads and legs from the shrimp, if desired, but leave on the tail shells. Place the sausage in a saucepan and cover with water. Bring to a boil and then simmer for 5 minutes. Drain and slice into ½-inch rounds. Set aside.

Heat the oil and fry the chicken pieces, browning evenly on both sides. Remove and drain on paper towels. Add the sausage, onions, garlic, and peppers to the oil in the skillet and fry briskly for about 3 minutes. Combine the sausage mixture with uncooked rice and saffron and place in a special Paella dish or a large oven- and flame-proof casserole. Pour on the water, season with salt and pepper, and bring to a boil. Stir occasionally and allow to boil for about 2 minutes. Add the chicken pieces and place in a preheated 400°F oven for about 15 minutes. Add the clams, mussels, shrimp, cod, and peas and cook a further 10-15 minutes or until the rice is tender, chicken is cooked, and mussels and clams open. Discard any that do not open. Add the tomatoes 5 minutes before the end of cooking time.

Time: Preparation takes 30-40 minutes and cooking takes 35-40 minutes.

Variation: Vary the ingredients to suit your own taste. Omit chicken or substitute pork for part of the quantity. Use Spanish or green onions if desired and add more sausage.

Crispy Fish with Chili

Choose your favorite white fish for this recipe.

SERVES 4

1 pound fish fillets, skinned, bones removed,
and cut into 1-inch cubes

Batter

½ cup all-purpose flour

1 egg, separated

1 Tbsp oil

6 Tbsps milk

Salt

Oil for deep frying

Sauce

1 tsp grated ginger root

¼ tsp chili powder

2 Tbsps tomato paste

2 Tbsps tomato chutney

2 Tbsps dark soy sauce

2 Tbsps Chinese wine or dry sherry

2 Tbsps water

1 tsp sugar

1 red chili, seeded and finely sliced

1 clove garlic, finely chopped

Salt and pepper

Sift the flour with a pinch of salt. Make a well in the center, and drop in the egg yolk and oil. Mix to a smooth batter with the milk, gradually incorporating the flour. Beat well. Cover and set aside in a cool place for 30 minutes.

Whisk egg white until stiff, and fold into batter just before using. Heat oil in wok. Dip fish pieces into batter and coat completely. When oil is hot, carefully lower fish pieces in until cooked through and golden brown – about 10 minutes. Remove with a slotted spoon. Reheat oil and refry each fish piece for 2 minutes. Remove with a slotted spoon and drain on paper towels.

Carefully remove all but 1 tablespoon of oil from the wok. Heat oil, add chili, ginger, garlic, chili powder, tomato paste, tomato chutney, soy sauce, sugar, wine, and water, and salt and pepper to taste. Stir well over heat for 3 minutes. Increase heat and toss in fish pieces. Coat with sauce and, when heated through, serve immediately.

Time: Preparation takes 40 minutes and cooking takes 30 minutes.

Monkfish Piperade

Monkfish is a wonderfully meaty firm-fleshed fish. If you cannot buy any, substitute another firm-fleshed white fish.

SERVES 4

1½ pounds monkfish fillets
2 onions
1 yellow bell pepper
1 red bell pepper
1 green bell pepper
1-2 cloves garlic
8 oz can tomatoes
Salt and pepper
2-3 Tbsps olive oil
1 small loaf French bread
Oil for deep frying

Slice onions thinly and soften in 1 tablespoon olive oil in a pan. Slice all the peppers in half, remove seeds, and cut into ½-inch strips. Mince the garlic and add to onions when tender, then cook gently for another 5 minutes. Add tomatoes and seasoning and simmer the sauce until the liquid has reduced by about half. If the fish fillets are large, cut them in half again lengthwise. Heat the remaining oil in a skillet and fry the fish until it is lightly brown. Transfer fish to an ovenproof dish, and when the piperade is ready, spoon it over the top of the fillets and heat through in a preheated 350°F oven for about 10 minutes. Meanwhile, slice the French bread on the diagonal into ½-inch slices. Fry in enough oil to barely cover until golden brown, then drain on paper towels. Put the monkfish piperade in a serving dish and surround with the bread.
Time: Preparation takes 20 minutes and cooking takes 30 minutes.

Fried Bass in — Cornmeal —

Cornmeal makes a crisp and subtly flavored coating for fried foods.

SERVES 4

2 cups yellow cornmeal
2 Tbsps all-purpose flour
Pinch of salt
2 tsps cayenne pepper
1 tsp ground cumin
2 tsps garlic granules
2 pounds freshwater bass or other whitefish fillets
Milk
Oil for deep frying
Lime wedges to garnish

Mix the cornmeal, flour, salt, cayenne, cumin, and garlic together in a shallow container or on a piece of wax paper. Skin the fillets if desired. Dip them into the milk and then lift to allow the excess to drip off. Place the fish in the cornmeal mixture and turn with two forks or, if using paper, lift the ends and toss the fish to coat. Meanwhile, heat oil in a deep skillet, large saucepan or deep-fat fryer. Add the fish in small batches and cook until the fillets float to the surface. Turn over and cook to brown lightly and evenly. Drain on paper towels and serve immediately with lime wedges.
Time: Preparation takes 20 minutes and cooking takes about 5 minutes.

Red Snapper with Nutmeg

For this original dish, zucchini "pancakes" are topped with sautéed fish fillets and served in a nutmeg-flavored cream sauce.

SERVES 6

2 red snappers weighing 2½ pounds each

8 zucchini

1 egg

1 Tbsp crème fraîche or sour cream

5 Tbsps olive oil

½ cup rich fish broth

1½ cups heavy cream

1 nutmeg

½ lemon

2 Tbsps butter

½ bunch chives, chopped

Salt and pepper

Cut the fins off the red snapper with a pair of scissors. Scrape off the scales with a fish scaler or the blade of a sharp knife. Clean the fish and rinse well. With a sharp knife, cut off the fillets, running the knife carefully down the backbone.

Using a vegetable grater, slice the zucchini into thin julienne. Discard the soft seed centre. In a bowl, beat the eggs with the crème fraîche, salt and pepper and then add the zucchini. Mix thoroughly with a fork. In a small ovenproof skillet, heat 1 tablespoon of oil and fry one-third of the zucchini mixture, flattening it into a pancake shape. After about 3 minutes turn over the zucchini galette and finish cooking it in a preheated 400°F oven. Repeat the process three times. Boil the broth until reduced by half, then stir in the heavy cream, 6 or 7 scrapings of nutmeg, salt, and pepper. Boil for 1 minute. Remove from the heat, blend smooth with a hand held electric blender, add a few drops of lemon juice and keep warm in a bowl of hot water.

Season the red snapper fillets with salt and pepper and a few scrapings of nutmeg. In 2 tablespoons of oil, melt the butter and fry the red snapper fillets for 2 minutes on both sides until lightly cooked. Finish cooking in a preheated 400°F oven for 8 minutes. The flesh will be firm and flake easily when cooked. Cut the galettes into 8 pieces, spread the pieces out on a plate, lay the fillets over and pour over the sauce. Sprinkle on the chopped chives.

Time: Preparation takes 1 hour and cooking takes 50 minutes.

Coulibiac

This is a variation of the classic Russian recipe.

SERVES 4

Pastry
4 cups all-purpose flour

4 sticks butter

⅔ cup iced water

1 egg, beaten

Filling
1 pound fresh salmon

4 small leeks, cleaned and trimmed

⅓ cup rice

2 hard-cooked eggs

4 Tbsps butter or margarine

8 oz mushrooms, sliced

2 Tbsps chopped fresh parsley

1 Tbsp chopped fresh thyme

Salt and pepper

Sauce
1¼ cups sour cream

¼ tsp grated horseradish

1 small bunch chives

Salt and pepper

Skin, trim, and bone the salmon, and cut into 4 equal-sized pieces. Cook rice until tender, rinse and set aside to cool. Cut leeks into lengths equal to those of the salmon, put them into a saucepan of cold water and bring to a boil. Cook until almost tender, drain, and allow to cool. Cook mushrooms for a few minutes in the butter. Add rice, parsley, thyme, and seasoning.

To prepare the pastry, cut the butter into ½-inch cubes. Sieve flour with a pinch of salt into a bowl and mix in cubed butter until it is well coated. Mix in the iced water, a little at a time, until the mixture just holds together. (The full quantity of water may not be needed.) Chill mixture for about 10 minutes. Turn the dough out onto a well-floured surface, shape it into a square and roll out to a rectangle 3 times as long as it is wide. Fold the bottom third of the dough up to the middle and the top third over it. Give the dough a half-turn, then roll out and fold again in the same way. Repeat the process once more, chilling the dough in between operations if the pastry gets too soft. Chill before using. Roll out the pastry to a square ¼-inch thick and cut into 4 even-sized pieces approximately 6-inch square. Save the trimmings. Brush each square with water and put a layer of the rice and mushroom mixture onto each. Place the cut pieces of leek on top of the rice, then put on another layer of rice. Cut the hard-cooked eggs in half and put one half on the rice layer. Add another layer of rice and, finally, the salmon piece. Fold the pastry over the salmon like an envelope and seal the edges well. Turn the envelope over and put onto a lightly-oiled cookie sheet. Brush each parcel with lightly beaten egg and cut the pastry trimmings into shapes to decorate the top. Brush these decorations with egg. Make a small hole in the center of each parcel. Bake in a preheated 400°F oven for 30 minutes. Meanwhile, prepare the sauce. Chop the chives and mix with the sour cream, horseradish, and seasoning. Just before serving, heat the sauce over a gentle heat. Do not allow to boil. Serve the sauce with the coulibiac and garnish with watercress, if desired.

Time: Preparation takes 30 minutes, cooking takes 30 minutes.

Shrimp Creole

The basis for this recipe is a spicy reddish-brown gravy that can be served with other meats such as chicken.

SERVES 4

4 Tbsps oil
1 large green bell pepper, cut into 1-inch pieces
2 stalks celery, sliced
2 medium onions, diced
2 cloves garlic, finely chopped
2 x 14 oz cans tomatoes
2 bay leaves
1 tsp cayenne pepper or Tabasco sauce
Salt and pepper
Pinch of thyme
2 Tbsps cornstarch mixed with 3 Tbsps dry white wine
1½ pounds shrimp, uncooked
Cooked rice, to serve

Heat the oil in a skillet and add the bell pepper, celery, and onions. Cook for a few minutes and add the garlic. Add the tomatoes and their juice, breaking them up with a fork. Add the bay leaves, cayenne pepper or Tabasco sauce, seasoning, and thyme, and bring to a boil. Simmer for about 5 minutes, uncovered. Mix a few spoonfuls of the hot tomato liquid with the cornstarch mixture and return it to the saucepan. Add the shrimp and cover the pan. Simmer for about 20 minutes, or until the shrimp look pink. Remove the bay leaves and serve the shrimp over hot rice.
Time: Preparation takes about 25 minutes and cooking takes 20-30 minutes.

Broiled Flounder

A mayonnaise-like topping puffs to a golden brown to give this mild-flavored fish a piquant taste.

SERVES 4

4 double fillets of flounder
2 eggs, separated
Pinch of salt, pepper, and dry mustard
1 cup peanut oil
4 Tbsps pickle relish
1 Tbsp chopped fresh parsley
1 Tbsp lemon juice
Dash of Tabasco sauce

Place the egg yolks in a blender, food processor or deep bowl. Blend in the salt, pepper, and mustard. If blending by hand, use a small whisk. If using the machine, pour the oil through the funnel in a thin, steady stream with the machine running. If mixing by hand, add oil a few drops at a time, beating well in between each addition. When half the oil has been added, the rest may be added in a thin steady stream while beating constantly with a small whisk.

Mix in the relish, parsley, lemon juice, and Tabasco sauce. Beat the egg whites until stiff but not dry and fold into the mayonnaise. Broil the fish about 2 inches from the heat source for about 6-10 minutes, or until the flesh looks opaque and flakes easily. Spread the sauce over each fillet and broil for 3-5 minutes longer, or until the sauce puffs and browns slightly.
Time: Preparation takes about 20 minutes and cooking takes 10-15 minutes.

Salmon Flan

This would make an excellent supper dish for four people.

SERVES 4-6

6 oz frozen puff paste

2 tsps cornstarch

²/₃ cup milk

Salt and pepper

6 oz cooked fresh salmon or 7½ oz can salmon

1 egg, lightly beaten

Dill for garnish

Thaw the pastry. Roll out into a square large enough to line a greased 8-inch quiche pan. Trim off the excess pastry and crimp the edges. Mix the cornstarch with 1 tablespoon of the milk, bring the rest to a boil, pour into the cornstarch mix, stir well, and return to the pan. Return to a boil and cook for 1 minute, stirring constantly. Season well with salt and pepper. If using canned salmon, drain the liquid from the can into the sauce. If using fresh salmon add 1 tablespoon butter.

Remove the pan from the heat and add the egg, beating it in thoroughly. Flake up the salmon, removing any bones and skin, fold it into the sauce and turn into the pie shell. Bake in a preheated 375°F oven for 35-40 minutes. Serve garnished with dill sprigs.

Time: Preparation takes 10 minutes and cooking takes 40-45 minutes.

Serving Idea: Serve either with a salad and brown bread and butter or with baked potatoes and petit pois.

Boston Scrod

This quick and easy dish is the perfect mid-week meal.

SERVES 4

4 even-sized scrod fillets
Salt and pepper
⅓ cup butter, melted
¾ cup dry bread crumbs
1 tsp dry mustard
1 tsp onion salt
Dash of Worcestershire sauce
Dash of Tabasco sauce
2 Tbsps lemon juice
1 Tbsp finely chopped fresh parsley

Season the fish fillets with salt and pepper and place them on a broiler tray. Brush with butter and broil for 3 minutes, or until just turning opaque. Combine the remaining butter with bread crumbs, mustard, onion salt, Worcestershire sauce, Tabasco sauce, lemon juice, and parsley. Spoon the mixture carefully on top of each fish fillet, covering it completely. Press down lightly to pack the crumbs into place. Broil for another 5-6 minutes, or until the top is lightly browned and the fish flakes easily.

Time: Preparation takes about 15 minutes and cooking takes 8-10 minutes.

Skate with Capers, Olives, & Shallots

The capers and shallots marry perfectly with the fish for a dish that is simply delicious

SERVES 4

4 wings of skate
1¼ cups white wine and water mixed
1 bay leaf
Salt
4 peppercorns
½ cup butter
2 shallots, chopped
2 Tbsps capers
½ cup pitted black olives, sliced
1 Tbsp chopped fresh mixed herbs
Lemon juice

Put the skate into a baking dish with the wine, water, bay leaf, salt, and peppercorns. Cover and poach in a preheated 350°F oven for 10 minutes, or until flesh looks opaque and flakes easily. Drain well, removing any skin, and keep warm. Melt the butter and cook the shallots quickly, to brown both. Add capers and olives and heat through. Add herbs and lemon juice. Pour over the skate and serve immediately.

Time: Preparation takes 10 minutes and cooking takes 15 minutes.

Stuffed Salmon Trout

Spinach, walnuts, and fresh herbs are combined to make a sophisticated stuffing for fish.

SERVES 6-8

1 fresh whole salmon trout, weighing 2½ pounds, cleaned
2 pounds fresh spinach
1 small onion
¼ cup margarine
½ cup walnuts, coarsely chopped
2 cups fresh white bread crumbs
1½ Tbsps chopped fresh parsley
1½ Tbsps chopped fresh thyme
Pinch of grated nutmeg
Salt and pepper
Juice of 2 lemons
Watercress sprigs and lemon slices, to garnish

Carefully cut the underside of the fish from the end of the slit made when the fish was cleaned, to the tip of the tail. Place the fish, belly side down, on a flat work surface, spreading the cut underside out to balance the fish more easily. Using the palm of your hand press down along the backbone of the fish, pushing the spine downwards towards the work surface. Turn the fish over and using a sharp knife, carefully pull the backbone away from the fish, cutting it away with scissors at the base of the head and tail. Remove the backbone completely and pull out any loose bones you may find with a pair of tweezers. Lay the boned fish in the center of a large square of lightly oiled aluminum foil and set aside.

Wash the spinach leaves well and tear off any coarse stalks. Put the spinach into a large saucepan and sprinkle with salt. Do not add any extra water. Cover and cook over a moderate heat for about 3 minutes. Turn the spinach into a colander and drain well, pressing with the back of a wooden spoon to remove all the excess moisture. Chop the cooked spinach very finely. Peel and chop the onion finely and fry gently in about 1 tablespoon of the margarine until soft, but not colored. Stir the cooked onion into the chopped spinach along with the walnuts, bread crumbs, herbs, nutmeg, salt, pepper, and half of the lemon juice. Mix well to blend evenly. Use the spinach stuffing to stuff the trout. Push the stuffing in firmly, re-shaping the fish as you do so. Allow a little of the stuffing to show between the cut edge of the fish. Seal the foil over the top of the fish, but do not wrap it too tightly.

Place the fish in a roasting pan and bake in a preheated 350°F oven for 35 minutes, or until the flesh flakes easily. Carefully unwrap the fish and transfer it to a large serving dish. Peel away the skin from all exposed sides of the fish. If possible remove some skin from the underside also. Whilst the fish is still hot, dot with the remaining margarine, sprinkle with the remaining lemon juice, then serve garnished with the watercress and sliced lemon.

Time: Preparation takes 35-40 minutes and cooking takes about 40 minutes.

Tuna Baked in — Parchment —

This recipe uses a French technique called "en papillote." Californians, quick to spot a healthful cooking method, use it often with fish.

SERVES 4

4 tuna steaks, about 8 oz each in weight
1 Spanish onion, thinly sliced
1 beefsteak tomato, cut in 4 slices
1 green bell pepper, cut in thin rings
8 large, uncooked peeled shrimp
2 tsps finely chopped fresh oregano
1 small green or red chili, seeded and finely chopped
4 Tbsps dry white wine or lemon juice
Salt
Oil

Lightly oil 4 oval pieces of baking parchment about 8x10 inches. Place a tuna steak on half of each piece of parchment and top with 2 slices of onion. Place a slice of tomato on each fish and top with the bell pepper rings. Place 2 shrimp on top and sprinkle over the oregano, salt, and chili pepper. Spoon the wine or lemon juice over each fish and fold the parchment over the fish. Overlap the edges and pinch and fold to seal securely. Place the parcels on a cookie sheet. Bake in a preheated 400°F oven for 10-12 minutes, or until flesh looks opaque and flakes easily. Unwrap each parcel at the table to serve.
Time: Preparation takes about 35 minutes and cooking takes 10-12 minutes.

Salmon & Fennel — Lasagne —

This unusual lasagne is mouthwatering!

SERVES 4

3 cups all-purpose flour, sifted
3 eggs, beaten
1 cup fairly runny white sauce
1¹⁄₃ pounds salmon (in one long strip if possible)
1 tsp fennel seeds
4 Tbsps grated cheese
1 cup fish broth
2 Tbsps butter
Salt and pepper

Make the dough by mixing together the flour, a good pinch of salt, and the 3 eggs. Set the dough aside to rest for 30 minutes and then roll out very thinly into long strips. Part-cook the pasta in salted, boiling water for 1 minute. Drain and then lay out on damp tea towels, without overlapping the strips.

Cut the salmon into thin slices and remove all the bones. Butter an ovenproof pan and place strips of pasta in the base. Now build up layers of white sauce, a few fennel seeds, the salmon, salt, pepper, and then another layer of pasta. Continue layering these ingredients until they are all used, finishing with a layer of pasta. Pour over the fish broth and then sprinkle over the cheese. Cook in a preheated 400°F oven for about 15-20 minutes, or until the fish broth has been almost completely absorbed.
Time: Preparation takes 40 minutes and cooking takes 35 minutes.

Crab Cakes with Red Pepper Sauce

The addition of bell peppers and herbs makes these crab cakes especially tasty.

SERVES 4

Red pepper sauce

4 plum tomatoes, peeled, seeded, and coarsely chopped

3 red bell peppers, roasted, peeled, seeded, and coarsely chopped

1 Tbsp tomato paste

3 Tbsps lemon thyme, chopped

Salt and pepper

Tabasco sauce

Lemon juice

Crab cakes

1 pound crab meat, picked over for shell particles

2 Tbsps finely chopped red bell pepper

2 Tbsps finely chopped yellow bell pepper

2 Tbsps finely chopped green bell pepper

2 Tbsps finely chopped celery

1 green onion, finely chopped

2 eggs

¼ cup dried bread crumbs

1 Tbsp fresh lemon thyme, chopped

1 Tbsp flat leaf parsley, chopped

1½ tsps coarse salt

¼ tsp fresh ground pepper

Zest of one lemon, grated

Butter

To serve

Sprigs of lemon thyme and corn kernels

To make the sauce, combine the tomatoes and peppers in a heavy-bottomed saucepan. Simmer over medium-low heat until they are very soft. Purée in a food processor, or pass through the fine blade of a food mill. Stir in the tomato paste and leave to cool. When cool, add the lemon thyme and season with salt and pepper, Tabasco sauce, and lemon juice to taste. Set aside.

Combine all the ingredients for the crab cakes, except for the butter, in a large bowl and mix well. Form the mixture into cakes 1½-inches in diameter and ½-inch thick. Sauté in butter over medium heat for approximately two minutes on each side, or until the cakes are lightly browned. To serve, place a spoonful of Red Pepper Sauce on each place. Arrange several crab cakes on top and garnish with lemon thyme and corn.

Time: Preparation takes about 35 minutes and cooking takes 20-25 minutes.

Sea Bass with Tomato Sauce

Sautéed fish fillets and a creamy tomato sauce combine with fennel to make an extra special dish.

SERVES 6

6 small sea bass

Juice of ½ lemon

1 Tbsp anise seed

3 Tbsps olive oil

3 fennel bulbs

2 cups milk

2 shallots

2 tomatoes

1½ cups rich fish broth

1 cup heavy cream

2 Tbsps butter

Fresh dill

Salt and pepper

Scale and clean the sea bass. Remove the fillets by cutting down the backbone. Cut each of the fillets in two to obtain 4 small fillets per person. Season with salt and pepper.

Mix together the lemon juice, anise seed and 2 tablespoons olive oil. Add the fish fillets and marinate for 1 hour, turning from time to time. Wash, trim, and slice the fennel. Discard the hard center core. Bring the milk to a boil. Add salt and the fennel slices and cook for 5 minutes. Drain, then spread on a kitchen towel to dry. Peel and finely chop the shallot. Cut the tomatoes in half and remove the seeds. Chop roughly. Drain the marinade into a skillet and add the shallots and tomato. Heat for 3 minutes, then add the fish broth. Reduce on a high heat for 5 minutes. When reduced, add the cream and bring to a boil. Remove from the heat and blend smooth with a hand held electric blender. Check seasoning. Strain the sauce through a fine sieve, pushing through with a spoon to obtain a smooth sauce. Keep warm over boiling water. Preheat a cast-iron griddle and grease it with a little oil. Sear the fish fillets on each side, beginning skin side down. Place in an ovenproof pan and cook in a preheated 400°F oven for 10 minutes, or until flesh looks opaque and flakes easily. Sauté the fennel in the remaining butter until lightly colored. Season with salt and pepper. Remove the fish from the oven. To serve, top the fennel with the fish and the sauce. Garnish with fresh dill.

Time: Preparation takes 40 minutes, plus 1 hour to marinate. Cooking takes 30 minutes.

Fisherman's Pie

This classic family meal is the perfect winter warmer.

SERVES 4-6

1 pound cod fillet
1 pound smoked cod or haddock fillet
¼ pint clams
½ cup peeled shrimp
1¼ cups milk
½ cup water
1 bay leaf
2 Tbsps butter
2 Tbsps all-purpose flour
2 Tbsps chopped fresh parsley
Squeeze of lemon juice
Salt and pepper

Topping
1½ pounds potatoes
1-2 Tbsps milk
2 Tbsps butter
Salt and pepper

Skin the fish and cut it into pieces. Keep fresh cod and smoked fish separate. Put it into a separate saucepan with milk, water, and half a bay leaf in each. Bring to a boil, lower heat and simmer, covered, for about 10 minutes until opaque. Meanwhile, peel potatoes and cut them into even-sized chunks. Add them to a pan of cold, salted water, bring to a boil and cook for about 20 minutes, or until tender. Drain, return to the hot saucepan and shake over heat until they are dry. Mash the potatoes, and beat in 2 or 3 tablespoons hot milk and half the butter. Season with salt and pepper and set aside. Remove the cooked fish from the milk and break it up, removing any bones. Strain cooking liquid from both saucepans – there should be about 1¼ cups in all. Melt butter in a saucepan over a low heat. Stir in the flour and cook gently for 1 minute. Gradually stir in the reserved fish liquid. Bring to a boil, stir well, and simmer for 2-3 minutes. Take off the heat, fold in the fish and parsley, and add lemon juice, salt and pepper, clams, and shrimp.

Butter an ovenproof dish and put the fish mixture in it. Fill a pastry bag, fitted with a rosette tube, with the mashed potato mixture and pipe in a lattice over the surface of the fish. Pipe a border round its edge. Dot over the remaining butter in pieces, and place in a preheated 375°F oven for about 20 minutes. Brown under a broiler, with grated cheese sprinkled on top, if desired.

Time: Preparation takes 20 minutes and cooking takes 45 minutes.

Herrings with Apples

The addition of apples complements the delicious and wholesome flavor of herring.

SERVES 4

4 herrings, cleaned

2 large dessert apples

1 large onion

4 large potatoes, peeled and sliced

Salt and pepper

½ cup dry cider

1 cup dried bread crumbs

¼ cup margarine

1½ Tbsps chopped fresh parsley

Cut the heads and tails from the herrings and split them open from the underside. Put the herrings, belly side down, on a flat surface and press along the back of each fish with the palm of your hand, pushing the backbone down towards the surface. Turn the herrings over and, with a sharp knife, carefully prise away the backbone, pulling out any loose bones as you go. Do not cut the fish into separate fillets. Wash and dry the fish well.

Peel, quarter, core, and slice one of the apples. Peel and slice the onion thinly. Lightly grease a shallow baking pan and layer with the potatoes, apple, and onions, seasoning well with salt and pepper between layers. Pour the cider over the potato layers and cover the dish with foil. Bake in a preheated 350°F oven for 40 minutes. Remove the dish from the oven and arrange the herring fillets over the top. Sprinkle the bread crumbs over the herrings and dot with half of the margarine. Increase the oven temperature to 400°F and return the dish to the oven for about 10-15 minutes, or until the herrings are cooked and brown. Core the remaining apples and slice into rounds, leaving the peel on. Melt the remaining margarine in a skillet and gently fry the apple slices. Remove the herrings from the oven and garnish with the fried apple slices and chopped parsley. Serve at once.

Time: Preparation takes 15-20 minutes and cooking takes about 50 minutes.

Variation: Use small mackerel instead of herrings in this recipe.

Halibut & Crab - Hollandaise -

This is a lovely sophisticated dish.

SERVES 4

4 large fillets of halibut
1 bay leaf
Slice of onion
5 Tbsps white wine
2 egg yolks
1 Tbsp lemon juice
Pinch of cayenne pepper and paprika
½ cup melted butter plus 1 Tbsp unmelted butter
2 Tbsps all-purpose flour
2 Tbsps heavy cream
8 oz crab meat

Put the fish with the bay leaf, onion slice, wine, and just enough water to cover the fish, into a baking dish. Cover and cook in a preheated 325°F oven for 10 minutes. Put the egg yolks, lemon juice, cayenne, and paprika into a food processor. Turn the machine on, gradually pour in the melted butter and process until thick. Set aside. Put the unmelted butter into a saucepan, melt over a gentle heat, and stir in the flour. Cook gently for 1 minute. Remove the fish from the baking dish and strain the cooking liquor onto the flour and butter, stirring well until the sauce is smooth and has thickened. Stir in the cream, but do not allow to boil. Season to taste. Stir the crab meat into the fish sauce and pour this mixture into a flameproof dish. Lay the halibut fillets on top and cover these with the Hollandaise sauce. Brown under a hot broiler before serving.
Time: Preparation takes 15 minutes, cooking takes 20 minutes.

Snapper with Orange — & Fennel —

Red snapper brings Florida to mind. Combined with oranges, it makes a lovely summer meal.

SERVES 4

Oil
4 even-sized red snapper, cleaned, heads and tails on
2 oranges
2 heads of fennel
Juice of 1 lemon
3 Tbsps light salad oil
Pinch of sugar, salt and pepper

Brush both sides of the fish with oil and cut three slits in the sides of each. Sprinkle with a little of the lemon juice, reserving the rest. Slice the fennel in half and remove the cores. Slice thinly. Also slice the green tops and chop the feathery herb to use in the dressing. Peel the oranges, removing all the white part. Cut the oranges into segments. Peel and segment over a bowl to catch the juice. Add lemon juice to any orange juice collected in the bowl. Add the oil, salt, pepper, and a pinch of sugar. Mix well and add the fennel, green herb tops, and orange segments, stirring carefully. Broil the fish 3-5 minutes per side, or until the flesh is opaque and flakes easily. Serve the fish with the heads and tails on, accompanied by the salad.

Time: Preparation takes about 30 minutes and cooking takes 6-10 minutes.
Cook's Tip: When broiling whole fish, make several cuts on the side of each fish to cook it quickly and evenly throughout.

Seafood Tart

This dish is a wonderful year-round meal because it can be adapted to include whatever seafood is in season.

SERVES 6-8

Pastry
2 cups all-purpose flour, sifted
½ cup unsalted butter
Pinch of salt
4 Tbsps cold milk

Filling
4 oz sole or cod fillets
8 oz cooked shrimp
4 oz crab meat
½ cup white wine
½ cup water
Large pinch of red pepper flakes
Salt and pepper
2 Tbsps butter
2 Tbsps all-purpose flour
1 clove garlic, finely chopped
2 egg yolks
½ cup heavy cream
Chopped parsley

To prepare the pastry, sift the flour into a bowl, cut the butter into small pieces and mix it into the flour until the mixture resembles fine bread crumbs. Make a well in the flour, pour in the milk, and add the salt. Mix with a fork, gradually incorporating the butter and flour mixture until all the ingredients are mixed. Form the dough into a ball and knead for about 1 minute. Leave the dough to cool in the refrigerator for about 1 hour.

To prepare the filling, cook the fish fillets in the wine and water with the red pepper flakes for about 10 minutes or until just firm to the touch. When the fish is cooked, remove it from the liquid and flake it into a bowl with the shrimp and the crab meat. Reserve the cooking liquid. Melt the butter in a small saucepan and stir in the flour. Gradually strain the cooking liquid from the fish, stirring constantly until smooth. Add garlic, place over high heat and bring to a boil. Lower the heat and allow to cook for 1 minute. Add to the fish in the bowl, season and set aside to cool.

On a well-floured surface, roll out the pastry and transfer it to a tart pan with a removable base. Press the dough into the pan and cut off any excess. Prick the base lightly with a fork and place a sheet of wax paper inside. Fill with rice, dried beans or baking beans and chill for 30 minutes. Bake the pastry shell in a preheated 375°F oven for 15 minutes. While the pastry is baking, combine the egg yolks, cream, and parsley and stir into the fish filling. Adjust the seasoning. Take the pastry shell out of the oven, remove the paper and beans, and pour in the filling. Return the tart to the oven and bake for another 25 minutes until lightly browned. Allow to cool slightly and then remove from the pan. Transfer to a serving dish and slice before serving.

Time: Preparation takes 40 minutes, plus 1 hour chilling. Cooking takes 40 minutes.

Index

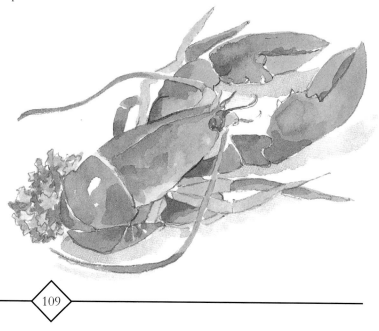